SpringerBriefs in Entrepreneurship and Innovation

Series Editors

David B. Audretsch
School of Public & Environmental Affair, Indiana University
Bloomington, IN, USA

Albert N. Link
Department of Economics, University of North Carolina at Greensboro
Greensboro, NC, USA

More information about this series at http://www.springer.com/series/11653

János Abonyi • Tímea Czvetkó
Gergely Marcell Honti

Are Regions Prepared for Industry 4.0?

The Industry 4.0+ Indicator System for Assessment

Springer

János Abonyi
Department of Process Engineering
University of Pannonia
Veszprém, Hungary

Tímea Czvetkó
University of Pannonia
Veszprém, Hungary

Gergely Marcell Honti
University of Pannonia
Veszprém, Hungary

ISSN 2195-5816 ISSN 2195-5824 (electronic)
SpringerBriefs in Entrepreneurship and Innovation
ISBN 978-3-030-53102-7 ISBN 978-3-030-53103-4 (eBook)
https://doi.org/10.1007/978-3-030-53103-4

This Springer imprint is published by the registered company Springer Nature Switzerland AG
The registered company address is: Gewerbestrasse 11, 6330 Cham, Switzerland

Preface

The aim of this book is to identify regional aspect of Industry 4.0 (I4.0+). The concept of I4.0 is spreading worldwide and readiness models exist to determine organisational or national maturity. However, the regional perspective of the digital transformation is neglected, although it significantly determines how the concept of Industry 4.0 can be introduced to the organisations. The major objective of this book is to provide a regional (NUTS 2 classified) I4.0-specific readiness model that can be widely used as it is based on solely open data sources.

Regional development serves as nutritious soil for digital transformation, so the proposed readiness model and the indicator system have been developed from the regional viewpoints of the actors of the triple helix model (Government, Business, Academia).

We build a region focused I4.0 indicator system, which is based on: (1) open governmental data; (2) alternative metrics of I4.0-related fields: graduates, study mobility programs, publications, density of institutions as well as patent applications; furthermore, (3) the GDELT Project (Global Data on Events, Location and Tone), which is one of the largest open databases that captures and categorises news and forms the connection between people, organisations, locations, themes, counts, images and emotions worldwide.

The constructed indicator system is analysed with the Sum of Ranking Differences (SRD) as well as the Promethee method and an I4.0+ composite indicator was developed based on the result of this analysis. The correlation of the resulted I4.0+ index with innovation (RII) and competitiveness (RCI) indexes indicates the importance of boosting regional I4.0 readiness and development.

The potential application areas of the developed I4.0+ index are also determined. The I4.0+ model and the indicators, and this book can serve as

- a tool to evaluate regional economy to support governmental decisions,
- a decision-support tool of territorial councils to define in which field they have to invest,

- a heat map for investors to determine which region has the potential of the successful implementation of I4.0 solutions, and what kind of co-operations should be enforced to ensure industry 4.0-friendly environment.

Acknowledgements

The work has been supported by the Hungarian Government through the Thematic Excellence Program (az NKFIH-1158-6/2019). The work of János Abonyi was supported by the European Union and co-financed by the European Social Fund through the project EFOP-3.6.2-16-2017-00017 entitled “Sustainable, intelligent and inclusive regional and city models”.

Veszprém, Hungary János Abonyi
Veszprém, Hungary Tímea Czvetkó
Veszprém, Hungary Gergely Marcell Honti
February 2020

Contents

Chapter 1
Introduction

In this rapidly changing environment, regions and cities are forced to develop their strengths in order to improve their overall competitiveness in an industrial environment [9]. Emerging technologies have already changed visions about manufacturing models, concepts or businesses [10]. Customer needs are constantly changing, so companies have to strive to satisfy demand. Businesses have to change their mindset not just according to manufacturing tools, but business models, strategies, data-driven services and employee qualifications as well. Through the ability to fast response to changes in the industry, companies can keep up and preserve their positions [5].

The fourth industrial revolution (Industry 4.0) is about including contemporary technologies of automation and real-time information exchange in manufacturing [8]. In this new phase, digital transformation is the primary driving force of competitiveness. Network-orientated production technologies can reduce reaction times, thus increasing productivity and flexibility.

We describe six main dimensions of the I4.0 concept based on the most widely applied I4.0 readiness model developed to evaluate how companies are ready for the digital transformation [2]. Table 1.1 shows the core concepts and the related requirements. We extended this table to show the key players that could help the companies in the development of the related competencies. As this analysis demonstrates, the fourth industrial revolution urges the cooperation of government, business sector, players of the education system , and research and development sector.

Industry 4.0 opens up new opportunities, not only for businesses, but the governments; collaborative territorial governance has to take a step forward to help small companies to apply Industry 4.0 as well as simultaneously develop the region itself [6].

It has been proven that to foster economic diversification and competitiveness, an innovation-based strategy of regions is essential [1]. In this knowledge-based economic system, knowledge in itself is insufficient to turn capabilities into eco-

J. Abonyi et al., *Are Regions Prepared for Industry 4.0?*, SpringerBriefs in Entrepreneurship and Innovation, https://doi.org/10.1007/978-3-030-53103-4_1

Table 1.1 The core dimensions of I4.0 and the appearance of supportive stakeholders

Dimension	Required features	Role
Strategy and organization		Government, R&D, Business
Strategy	Industry 4.0 strategy	
Investment	GERD, BERD, Patents	
Smart factory		Government, R&D, Business
Equipment	Integrated M2M	
Digital modelling	Automated, digital data collection	
Data usage	Used in all areas/activities	
IT systems	Integrated	
Smart operations		R&D and Business
Cloud computing	Cloud-based software, data storage and analytics	
IT security	Internal data storage	
Automatization	Self-reacting processes	
Information sharing	in production, finance, sales, IT, R&D, logistics	
Smart products		R&D, Business
Data analytics in usage phase	Product development	
	Comprehensive usage of collected data	
Data-driven services		R&D, Business
	Through customer integration	
	High usage rate of data	
Employees		Government, Education, Business
	PhD colleagues, Dual degree students	
	Training, knowledge transfer system, life long learning (LLL)	

nomic development, the participation of institutions is also needed [3]. Figure 1.1 introduces the key stakeholders and their role in supporting the dynamics of competitiveness and regional development. Our study strongly focuses on the triple helix model, as all the three sectors attendance (government, business, academia) are responsible in creating a competitive environment, e.g. the academic sector is the key of knowledge, the core potential of innovation, while the government is responsible to ensure stable interactions [7]. In the light of this concept, the represented synergies and collaboration between them (university, industry and government) can be a leading path towards emerging and innovative regions [1].

It can be stated that I4.0 functioning as a strategy for economic development by utilizing potentials in digital transformation. This study aims to identify the effect of various factors of the implementation of Industry 4.0 at a regional level.

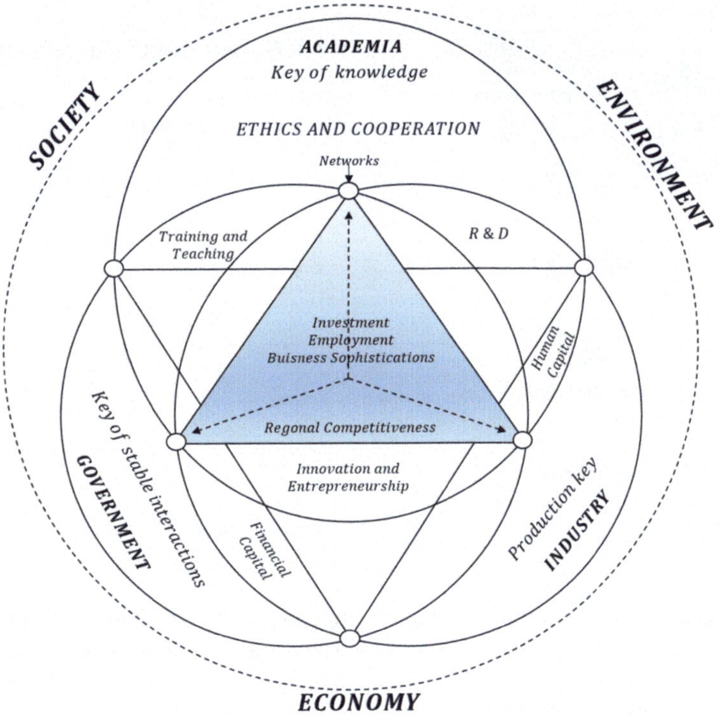

Fig. 1.1 Triple helix model, the concept of regional competitiveness and development [4]

We overview of what are the key elements that influence the ability to create a technology-oriented environment. Several readiness indexes are connected to the development of Industry 4.0, which focus its internal conditions more precisely. In order to build a more stable focus, in this book, we also take into consideration the external factors and their impact on the companies and regional development.

Figure 1.2 reflects the methodology of how we developed the Industry 4.0 readiness concept and indicator system. However organizational and nationwide I4.0 readiness models are exists, the regional aspect is out-of focus. In the light of the aforementioned, the Industry 4.0+ is presented as a concept which crosses over sectoral boundaries as well as serve as a base unit of territorial resource-transfer (knowledge, interaction, production, labour). The aim of this book is to provide a region-specific (NUTS 2 classified) Industry 4.0 readiness concept (I4.0+), which measures are based on solely open data.

In this regard, firstly we review the Industry 4.0-based regional development factors and their effects in Sect. 2. Secondly, regional indicators and their connections to the concept of I4.0 are interpreted in Sect. 3. Section 4 overviews the generated composite indicators based on open data. In Sect. 4.3 the conclusion of the study is

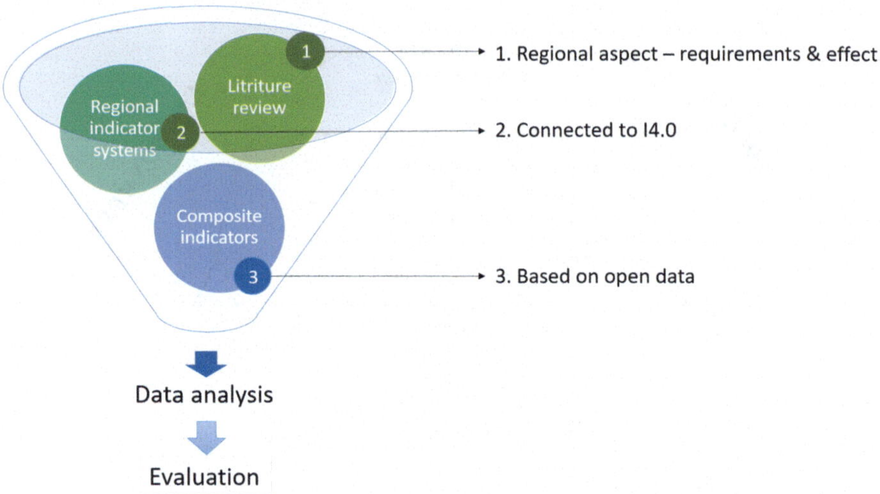

Fig. 1.2 Dimensions of an I4.0-specific regional readiness evaluation

presented by an application study of the European Union, while the correlations with relevant indicators is discussed in Sect. 4.4. The priority of creating this concept is to ease and help decision making processes. The possible stakeholders and application fields are interpreted in Sect. 5.

References

1. Asheim, B. T. (2019). Smart specialisation, innovation policy and regional innovation systems: What about new path development in less innovative regions? *Innovation: The European Journal of Social Science Research, 32*(1), 8–25.
2. Bertenrath, R., Blum, M., Bleider, M., Millack, A., Schmitt, K., Schmitz, E., et al. (2015). *Industrie 4.0 readiness*. Impuls-Stiftung.
3. Carayannis, E., & Grigoroudis, E. (2016). Quadruple innovation helix and smart specialization: Knowledge production and national competitiveness. *Foresight and STI Governance (Foresight-Russia till No. 3/2015), 10*(1), 31–42.
4. Compagnucci, L., & Spigarelli, F. (2018). Fostering cross-sector collaboration to promote innovation in the water sector. *Sustainability, 10*(11), 4154.
5. Duarte, S., do Rosário Cabrita, M., & Cruz-Machado, V. (2019). Business model, lean and green management and industry 4.0: A conceptual relationship. In: *International Conference on Management Science and Engineering Management* (pp. 359–372). Berlin: Springer.
6. Larrea, M., Estensoro, M., & Sisti, E. (2018). The contribution of action research to industry 4.0 policies: Bringing empowerment and democracy to the economic efficiency arena. *International Journal of Action Research, 14*, 164–180.
7. Monostori, L., Váncza, J., Várgedő, T., Lengyel, L., Varjta, L., Henter, Á., et al. (2016). *Ipar 4.0 cselekvési terv*.

8. Peraković, D., Periša, M., & Zorić, P. (2019). Challenges and issues of ict in industry 4.0. In *Design, simulation, manufacturing: The innovation exchange* (pp. 259–269). Berlin: Springer.
9. Ruohomaa, H., & Salminen, V. (2018). Regional development in modern robotic education on industrial and society context. In *International Conference on Applied Human Factors and Ergonomics* (pp. 159–168). Berlin: Springer.
10. Zhong, R. Y., Xu, X., Klotz, E., & Newman, S. T. (2017). Intelligent manufacturing in the context of industry 4.0: A review. *Engineering, 3*(5), 616–630.

Chapter 2
Regional Aspects of Industry 4.0

2.1 The Dimensions of Industry 4.0

The analysis of I.40 readiness models reveal the focus areas which need to be considered within an organization in terms of a successful adaption of I4.0. Table 2.1 below represents the reviewed readiness models and their focus area to provide an outline of the topics that we will discuss. Some factors mentioned by the majority of authors, e.g. the role of people as well as employees and their relationship with emerging technologies, strategies and leadership in the case of companies or in terms of technology. Some overlaps exist between the aforementioned factors, although it is sometimes evident that less articles concern the role of governments or the intensity of innovation (however, this may apply in a different dimension).

It should be noticed that these models reflect the perspective of the companies, the perspective of regional development is missing even though this has a significant effect on both companies and countries.

To handle this problem we transform the internal aspects of I4.0 readiness into external conditions. This concept is formed in accordance with our vision concerning the necessary economic environment, which can be nutritious soil for I4.0. As it is shown in Tables 2.2–2.3, we categorized the elements of the readiness model according to their connection to the main fostering groups of regional development.

The primary aim of our work is to determine indicators which are externally able to measure the readiness of regions. For example, we can identify innovation intensity by research activities, investments in development or cross-collaboration activities. These are measurable by different indicators described in Tables 2.2–2.3, in terms of the density of patent applications or in the form of innovative collaborations between small and medium-sized enterprises (SMEs).

J. Abonyi et al., *Are Regions Prepared for Industry 4.0?*, SpringerBriefs in Entrepreneurship and Innovation, https://doi.org/10.1007/978-3-030-53103-4_2

Table 2.1 Review of readiness models (1- Strategy, 2- Leadership, 3- Customers, 4- Operations, 5- Products, 6- Culture, 7- People, 8- Governance, 9- Technology,10- Value creation, 11- Data and information, 12- Corporate standards, 13- Production, 14- Critical areas, 15- Innovation intensity, 16- Smart factory, 17-Collaboration, 18- Performance and enablement, 19- Outcome)

Authors	Name	Year	Dimensions	For	1	2	3	4	5	6	7	8	9	10	11	12	13	14	15	16	17	18	19
Impuls	Industrie 4.0 Readiness [2]	2015	6	SMEs	X			X	X		X		X		X					X			
Roland Berger	Think Act Industrie 4.0 [3]	2015	2	Country							X		X	X			X		X				
Andreas Schumacher et al.	A maturity model for assessing Industry 4.0 readiness and maturity of manufacturing enterprises [27]	2016	9	SMEs	X	X	X	X	X	X	X	X	X										
G. Nick, and Ferenc Pongrácz	How to measure Industry 4.0 readiness of cities [23]	2016	3	Cities							X	X	X								X	X	X
Viharos, Z. J. et al.	Non-comparative, Industry 4.0 Readiness Evaluation for Manufacturing Enterprises [34]	2017	8	SMEs	X	X	X	X		X	X		X				X	X					
Andreas Schumacher et al.	Roadmapping towards industrial digitalization based on an Industry 4.0 maturity model for manufacturing enterprises [28]	2019	8	SMEs	X	X	X	X			X		X	X	X	X							
Dennis Trotta and Patrizia Garengo	Assessing Industry 4.0 Maturity: An Essential Scale for SMEs [32]	2019	5	SMEs	X			X			X		X				X						

Table 2.2 Industry 4.0 readiness internal factors' categorized into necessary external conditions, completed with measuring techniques. (HE- Higher Education, LM- Labour Market, INO- Innovation, INV- Investment, TECH- Technology)

No.	Internal factors	External conditions	Category	Measure
1	Strategy	Assisting SMEs	LM	Expenditures on assisting SMEs and the craft sector
			LM	No. of SMEs in regions
		RIS3 policy	LM/INO/HE	S3 strategy implementation
		Creative cities and sustainable regions	HE/LM/INO/INV/TECH	KRAFT index[21]
2	Leadership	Aspiration for development	INO/LM	Business Enterprises Expenditure on R&D (BERD)
3	Customer	Opennes to new technologies	TECH	No. of people ordering via Internet
4	Products	Manufacturing enterprises	LM	No. of manufacturing SMEs
5	Operations	Cross collaboration	INO/LM	Innovative SMEs collaborating with others
			LM/INO/HE	S3 strategy implementation
6	Culture	Tone of I4.0-related news	HE/LM/INO/INV/TECH	Density of news (judgement + or −)
7	People	Well-qualified workforce	LM	No. of students finishing university in IT, Engineering, Mathematics
		Ability for Lifelong learning	LM/HE	Population aged 25–64 by educational attainment
8	Governance	Industry supportive policies	INV	European Policies for regional development
		Financial support	INV/INO	Gross Domestic Expenditure on R&D (GERD)
			INV	European Fund expenditure on regions
9	Technology	Technological adaption	TECH/INV	Expenditures on telecommunication infrastructure and information society
			TECH/INV	Expenditures on technical assistance and innovative actions
		Workforce qualification	HE	No. of students finishing university in IT
10	Value creation	Technological adaption	TECH/INV	Expenditures on telecommunication infrastructure and information society
			TECH/INV	Expenditures on technical assistance and innovative actions
		Workforce qualification	HE	No. of students finishing university in IT, Engineering, Mathematics

Table 2.3 (continued) Industry 4.0 readiness internal factors' categorized into necessary external conditions, along with measuring techniques. (HE- Higher Education, LM- Labour Market, INO- Innovation, INV- Investment, TECH- Technology)

No.	Internal factors	External conditions	Category	Measure
11	Data and information	Cloud computing	TECH	Expenditures on technical assistance and innovative actions
12	Corporate standards	Support lifelong learning	LM/HE	Population aged 25–64 by educational attainment
		Cross collaboration activities	INO/LM	Innovative SMEs collaborating with others
			LM/INO/HE	S3 strategy implementation
13	Production	Medium-high and high-tech manufacturing	LM/TECH	Employment in medium-high/high-tech manufacturing and knowledge-intensive
		Manufacturing enterprises	LM	No of manufacturing SMEs
14	Critical areas	Regional development	HE/LM/INO/INV/TECH	Regional Innovation Scoreboard (RIS) [20]
			HE/LM/INO/INV/TECH	Regional Competitiveness Index (RCI) [25]
		Creative cities and sustainable regions	HE/LM/INO/INV/TECH	KRAFT index [21]
		Cultural and creative cities	HE/LM/INO/INV/TECH	C3 monitoring [15]

15	Innovation intensity	Research and development activities	INO	Density of patent applications
			INO	No. of scientific publications
		Cross collaboration activities	INO/LM	Innovative SMEs collaborating with others
			LM/INO/HE	S3 strategy implementation
		Investment in development	INV/INO	R&D expenditures (GERD, BERD)
			INV/INO	Expenditures on research, technological development and innovation (RTDI)
			INV/INO	Total R&D personnel and researcher
		Job opportunities	INO/LM	No. of persons employed in professional, scientific and technical activities
			INO/LM	Density of research institutions
		Creative cities and sustainable regions	HE/LM/INO/INV/TECH	KRAFT index [21]
16	Smart factory	Smart environment	TECH	Smart city index

2.2 Essential Factors and Impacts of I4.0 Based Regional Development

2.2.1 Factors of Horizontal Integration

In order to create an I4.0 system, organizations must also take into consideration technical and social challenges. "The successful adoption of the 4th industrial revolution will rely on the ability of governments, business and citizens to commit in supporting the transformation of society into a modern and smart a society-driven by advanced technology, skills, innovation and responsive policy" [17].

From a technical point of view, digital transformation is an essential requirement, so the aforementioned disruptive technologies can build on this.

I4.0 needs to apply three distinct types of integration as is shown in Fig. 2.1.

Firstly, horizontal integration, which means collaboration between stakeholders, is redound to create a productive ecosystem that grants the flow of material, information, energy and finance [7]. Secondly, the hierarchical integration of the IT system from manufacturing through to logistics and sales. The aim is to create flexible and cross-functional collaboration [13]. End-to-end digital integration of engineering throughout the value chain to facilitate the consistent and customer-oriented usage of product model [7].

Considering the economic/financial background of I4.0, digital adaption requires high initial rates of investment. According to research, 36 per cent of companies are afraid of the high costs and 38 per cent are uncertain about the economic pay-off [22].

The challenge is not simply the selection of a suitable technology, but also the lack of digital culture and skills at the given organization. Organizations have to change their attitude according to the requirements of I4.0 and communication about changes. This requires a high degree of flexibility, short periods of development and innovation, resource efficiency, decentralization and accelerate decision-making. If a company can meet its requirements, productivity can be intensified [13].

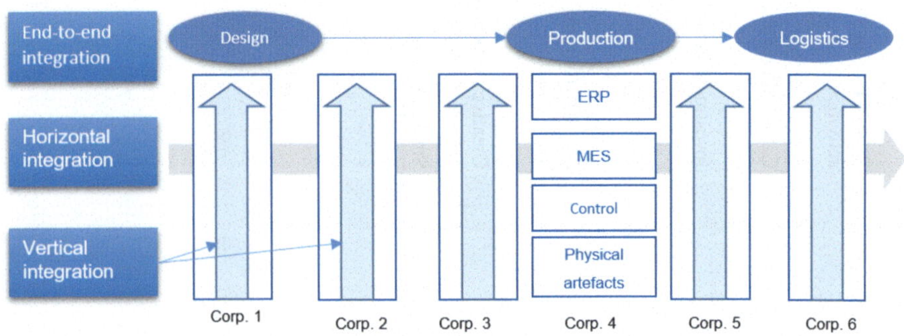

Fig. 2.1 The advantage of the horizontal integration [35]

Furthermore, companies should make their staff understand how the organization will go through changes and how they are effected. Companies that invest in building a digital culture need to ensure that their leaders communicate changes clearly and comprehensibly [9].

It must also be ensured, that this aspect is beyond the perspective of companies; it carries the glocal aspect and values through processes and innovative value chains. By the utilization of spatial interconnections as well as cooperation with external parties like universities, other companies or the government, a better functioning and more competitive environment can be consciously built.

In this regards, technology is one of our segments that is measured by indicators so that they can reveal regional readiness. On the one hand, our intention was to measure the expenditures of adapting technological developments. Although as was previously mentioned collaboration activities play a significant role and people must be able to adapt to these changes and have the skills demanded. This is why the collaboration of SMEs with others and the potential ability of people for lifelong learning. On the other hand, the attitude of people towards new technological development and the concept of I4.0 is a relevant factor with regard to the measurement of readiness.

2.2.2 Education and Its Connection to Changes in the Labour Market

Due to the progression of digital transformation and innovation, the labour market is being transformed and industry will demand an immensely skilled labour force with new skill sets [17].

According to a report from the World Economic Forum (WEF), between 23 per cent and 37 per cent of companies are planning to invest in robotization between 2018 and 2022 (the percentage differs among sectors) [37]. This indicates that certain types of jobs may be displaced, although it is claimed that a higher output and productivity can be balanced or even outweigh job displacement [14]. According to the WEF report, on the one hand, the change in the division of labour between humans and machines will result in the displacement of 75 million jobs, while on the other hand, 133 million new jobs will be created through new occupations and industries [37].

Institutions and governments are under constant pressure to identify new skill development models to ensure job opportunities for those of working age [14]. Furthermore, it is challenging for businesses, governments and individuals to foresee the future demand for skills and job content effect on the workforce.

Figure 2.2 represents the relationship between the stakeholders (Business, Education, Government) in connection with the processes of skill development.

In order to generate creativity and an innovative environment, the triple helix actors and both the soft factors play a significant role. A possible solution is to

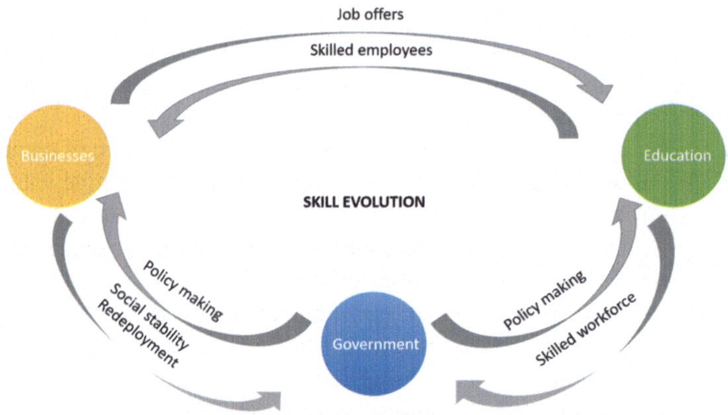

Fig. 2.2 The relationship between skill development-related stakeholders

provide new knowledge by creating knowledge centres, institutions which offer the basis of interconnections and knowledge flow. This would amplify its effect by connecting with high-tech infrastructure [21]. However, it must be noted that no industry is purely creative, although such have been developed and transformed throughout history [29].

On the other hand, the role of government in the case of skill evolution and innovation can be realized through education and labour-related policymaking. However, collaboration between businesses and governments is necessary in order to solve the problem of cost concerns, maintain social stability and redeploy redundant skills between sectors. For businesses, it has the potential to enter new markets, providing new services for customers, entrepreneurs, corporations or the public sector. This might create a new source of employment. It is getting harder to identify talents; that is why talent management as well as proactive and innovative skill building is a pressing issue.

Two spatial articulations of the politics of labour exist: the macro- and micropolitical frames. The former claims that skill is a classificatory schema which divides and locates labour in a discrete space. On the other hand, in terms of micropolitics, it "occurs through a dynamic space of ongoing transitions in enablement and constraint that produce workers through the contingencies of their working environment" [26].

The essential purpose of the needed skills is to ensure that people are flexible and able to adapt to rapid changes. The new demand for skills requires the employee to have both technical and social skills complemented with an analytic mindset [36].

Three types of skills can be distinguished which are becoming more critical in the labour market of the fourth industrial revolution, namely advanced cognitive skills, socio-behavioural skills and skill combinations [30] (see Fig. 2.3).

As has already been highlighted, workforce competency is appreciated and calls for increasing lifelong-learning activities. The emerging trend of digitalization is changing the way of communication and learning. The expectation of new learning

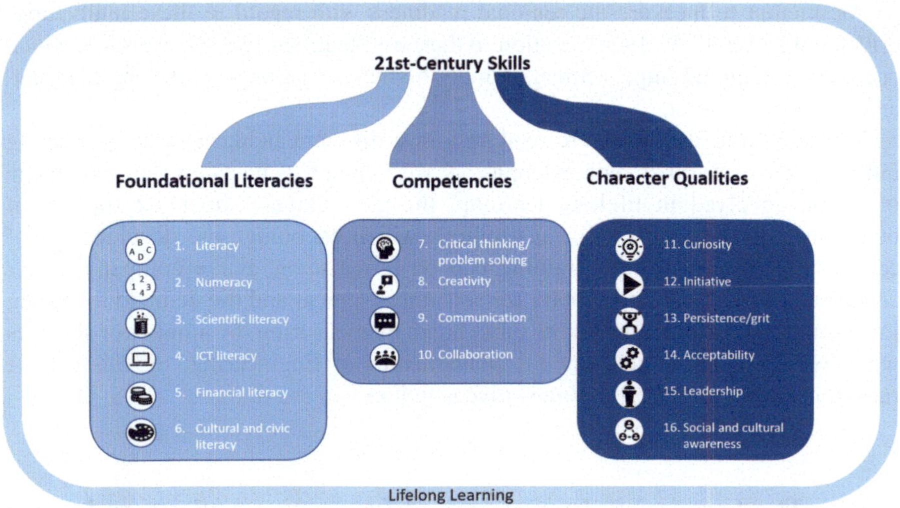

Fig. 2.3 Essential skills demanded for a competitive future [36]

requires to be continuous, on-demand and "takes place in short bursts and on the go and in the flow of work". Moreover, it should originate from a personal motivation to adapt to changing demands [33]. This would result in a wholesale reskilling of the workforce, which means that even with the transformation of the labour market, people can cope with the challenging situation presented by a new kind of job creation. Partnerships between businesses, educational institutions and accreditation providers might result in a significant increase in the "quality of talent pool" [36].

"Whenever the industrial structure becomes more advanced and rational, the demand for advanced talents emerges within a short time period". It is also claimed that a strong relationship exists between upgrading the industrial structure and educational advancement [12]. "Meanwhile, the advent of the global economy, the expansion of technological knowledge, and the growth of knowledge production have made higher education inclusive and directly responsible for the evolution of industrial structure." [12]. In this relation, the role of universities is significant. Universities generate new knowledge, so as companies seek to collaborate with academic research groups, for universities this is a great possibility to expand their role in economic development in their region. It is said to be a driver of regional economic development. After identifying the needs and peculiarities of the region, universities can have an important effect in rebounding socio-economic development with studies, education, innovation or infrastructure development [38].

In light of the above, the relationship between education and the labour market is inevitably becoming stronger as both have a deep dependence from the governmental support for development. All these segments are going through a massive change in the fields of perception and enforcement.

We attempt to measure the regional readiness with regard to these innovation-driven transformations. In connection to that, we identified two other groups which bring about regional improvement, namely higher education and lifelong learning, and the labour market.

Indicators aimed to measure readiness in a different field, have an interacting influence on each other. For example, as we attempt to measure the percentage of people involved in lifelong learning, the governmental financial support of both educational and industrial institutions which encourage the development of education and/or vocational training can be relied upon. For a company, better conditions provide the opportunity for self-improvement and the demand for filling job vacancies will increase. On the other hand, by measuring the number of students who graduated in the fields of IT, Mathematics or Engineering, regions can be ranked in terms of supporting innovative activities.

2.2.3 The Increasing Importance of Innovative Actions and Collaborations

The fourth Industrial Revolution has led to an appreciation of the importance of research and development (R&D) and become the basis of innovation. Innovation capability is being addressed as a critical component of I4.0 because it empowers the ability of a company or region to be competitive [17]. Innovation can only be maintained by the actors of the triple helix model because the responsibility of budget allocation for R&D can not be in only one hand. The involvement of universities, firms and the state can lead to the provision of a new kind of knowledge in companies [31].

Nowadays, traditional R&D institutions are being transformed and developed, in order to ameliorate the connection and interaction with their industry. "In this context, the Triple Helix institution actors, university, industry, R&D institutions and government can be interpreted as an innovative, entrepreneurial ecosystem with the interactive relationships from different institutional spheres" [8].

Innovation processes can occur through the usage of new technologies, but on the other hand, one of the most critical activities is to generate new ideas [24].

Those organizations which only focus on the improvement of existing services or processes are unable to adapt to environmental changes. Otherwise, these companies can make the most out of their activities, which create structural ambidexterity with the allocation of different units that focus on exploitation as well as exploration [24].

The use of industrial internet platforms has led to the transformation of the control of data, information and knowledge in the whole product lifecycle, access and management. Product lifecycle management (PLM) focus on the efficient use of data, information and knowledge in product development and value creation for customers [1].

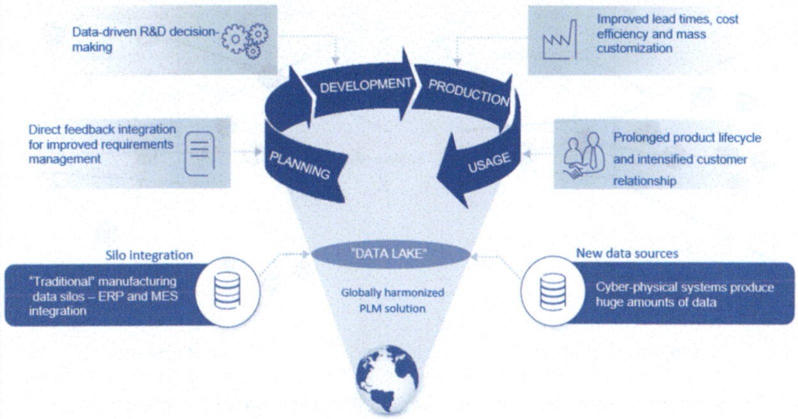

Fig. 2.4 PLM supportive innovative actions [1]

Figure 2.4 refers to the innovation-driven technologies and processes, which can provide real-time realization of data resulting in a more open and effective management of product lifecycles [19].

Following changes to product lifecycles, the reaction time to market has been accelerating along with the need for innovation.

It is assumed, that ecosystem based open collaboration model creates a suitable environment for I4.0 enablement [23].

The difference between closed and open innovation systems is rooted in the utilization of external sources and the perception of opening up to opportunities. Figure 2.5 illustrates the aforementioned concept.

Open innovation can be regarded as a new approach to innovation, an externalized form of it. Innovation and investment are observed in the long run to face problems and to handle the challenges by developing short-term tactics. Open innovation goes far beyond specific tactics for boosting competitiveness; it can be determined as a "part of an emergent system of overarching governance" [5].

Open innovation goes beyond a company, as it is belied that external knowledge and resources can accelerate as well as improve innovation itself. In this concept, customers are involved and the shortened product life-cycle can be assessed more precisely. Thanks to open innovation, external parties, e.g. universities, research organizations or national government can increase the efficiency of finding solutions to innovation and sustainability-related challenges [18].

Regarding the perspective aforementioned, we have to bear in mind the regional and national interactions, as well as the importance of determining the factors that effect on national development through regional technological innovation. In connection to this, regions are hardly able to develop without governmental support. Policymaking for utilizing activities driven by industrial growth is essential factors to boost economic development as a whole.

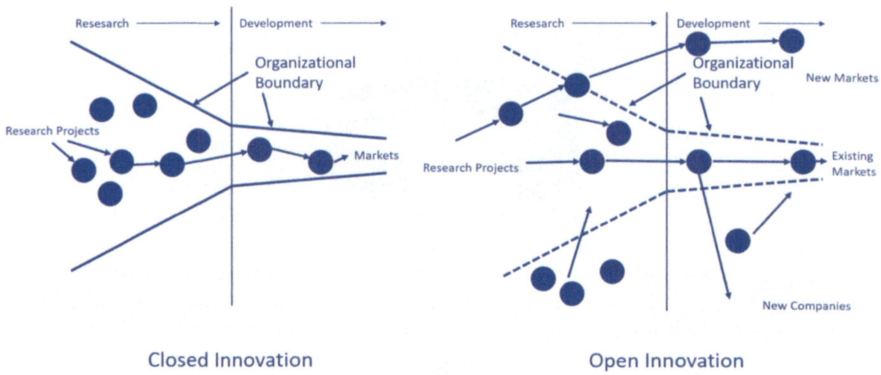

Fig. 2.5 The potential of open innovation collaborating with external parties [16]

Innovation is also a major force of regional development. It interweaves all the sectors, namely technology, higher education and lifelong learning, the labour market and last but not least, investment. According to those involved in higher education and lifelong learning, it is assumed that the number of knowledge workers is going to increase and become involved in the creative and knowledge-intensive sectors of the labour market. While the innovative collaboration between businesses can indicate the regional perception of open innovation, especially if it is complemented with financial support from the government and/or businesses. The number of research institutions, patent applications and publications in the field of I4.0 can be indicative of the innovation capability of a given region.

2.3 Policies and Funds Supporting Regional Development

In this section, we are discussing some relevant policies, which support the competitiveness and development of the EU/regions/industries. A certain level of development is required in order to be able to implement Industry 4.0 successfully. On the other hand, Industry 4.0 can be the driving force of innovation and development, as it can boost the regions and their surroundings' competitiveness.

The interaction between local and non-local factors results in the advancement of industries and regional economies. The roles of regional and cluster-related regional policies have changed on account of the expansion of globalization, which has resulted in a shift in interaction from local to a global level. It is claimed that industry- or firm-related factors can be a driving force of cluster development. Although cluster policies must consider the "industry life cycle" as the early stage of the industry, the local forces have higher relevance, while as the industry matures, the global position gains importance [11].

Fig. 2.6 The European Commission's Investment Plan for a competitive Europe (EC IPE) [6]

The European Commission has implemented several policies and provided funding for a more innovative, competitive and healthier Europe. In Fig. 2.6, a list of sources of investment in the field is given.

"A strong industrial base will be of key importance for Europe's economic recovery and competitiveness" [4]. The industrial sector has been the target over the last few years, as it is expected to be the driver of innovation, jobs, growth and wealth. Industry accounts for more than 80 per cent of both exports and in Europe as well as private research and innovation [4].

The overall aim of Europe is to be innovative, sustainable and achieve continuous progress. There is an urgent need for analytical tools, which enable innovation ecosystems as well as their determinants, namely maturity and structural development, to be assessed [10].

Table 2.4 outlines those European initiatives which aim to strengthen economic growth and foster innovation-driven development. The table is not conclusion specific. We examined their relation to our five areas mentioned. Innovation is aimed to be the driving force, which is helping the labour market to create job opportunities according to new demands. All the areas are related to industry and facilitating the adaptation of the concept of I4.0.

As can be seen, most of the initiatives timely "end" in 2020, although it is worth noticing that applications and investments yield a return over the following 1–3 years.

Beyond governmental support, a concept of the adapted areas and fields can be created. As an example, the allocation of financial support between regions can be indicative of the aspiration to improve. Furthermore, the Smart Specialisation

Table 2.4 Policies that foster development and financial funds from the European Union

	Name	Year	Kind of support	For whom	Aim	Higher education & LLL	Labour market	Technology	Innovation	Investment
1	Horizon 2020	2014–2020	Financial	Europe	Securing Europe's global competitiveness	Indirect	X	X	X	X
2	Industrial renais-sance	2014–2020	Policy	European countries and regions	Boost in industry for creating jobs and growth	X	X	X	X	X
3	European fund for strategic invest-ments	2014–2020	Financial	Companies of all sizes, utilities, national banks, the public sector and investment funds	Aims to overcome current market failures by addressing market goals and mobilising private investment	X	X	X	X	X
4	Industry 2030 high level industrial roundtable	2019–2030	Policy	Europe	In 2030, industry in Europe will be a global leader that will responsibly deliver value for society, the environment and the economy	X	X	X	X	X

5	New cohesion policy	2021–2027	Policy	Regional, SMEs	It targets all regions and cities in the European Union in order to support job creation, business competitiveness, economic growth, sustainable development, and improve the quality of life of citizens	X	X	X	X	X
6	Cluster policy		Policy	National and regional	The European Observatory for Clusters and Industrial Change (EOCIC) provides policy support to existing or emerging cluster initiatives at the national and regional levels		X		X	
7	Smart speciali-sation platform (S3P)		Policy	Regions, inter-cluster cooperation	Combine smart specialisation and interregional cooperation to boost industrial competitiveness and innovation			X	X	
8	European regional develop-ment fund		Financial	Regions	The ERDF aims to strengthen economic and social cohesion in the European Union by correcting imbalances between its regions		X	X	X	X

Strategy (S3) can identify a regional innovation capability and even be monitored by companies, which may help with regard to decision-making in the field of investment or collaboration.

2.4 The Presence of RIS3 Strategy in Regional Growth and Innovation

It is claimed that there is a higher chance of success for those strategies which are able to combine the innovation features with specific regional strengths. Smart Specialisation Strategy (S3)[1] is seeking to utilize the unique assets, resources and potential by relying on the regional structure and knowledge bases. S3 beyond fostering research and innovation capability, is aimed to stimulate the partnership within the quadruple helix (public entities—knowledge institutions—businesses—civil society) and to help regions to cope with societal challenges and non-science oriented innovation as well. Although Research and Innovation Strategies for Smart Specialisation (RIS3) requires a structural and place-based economic transformation. Government authority is to coordinate and synchronize the collaboration of the partners and resources within the quadruple helix.

This strategy can be applied for any regions, even regions have various ecosystems, knowledge production as well as different paths for growing opportunities. Taking advantage of regions and industries similarity/complementary, interregional collaborations can drive economic growth and competitiveness. On the other hand, cultural and creative cities and regions remarkable impact on smart and sustainable growth cannot be dismissed as well as that the EU 2020 Strategy potential in financing development plans.

For boosting regional development, science and technology parks (STPs)[2] can be effective instruments to implement. The implementation of STPs aime to bring innovative features and technology-based activities by the utilization of potential in collaboration of science and industry as well as determine localised development goals. The role of STPs connected to regional development, can approached from two perspective, namely interactive view or innovation ecosystem perception. According to the former, STPs interact as facilitators in a placed-based transfer system, while the latter address a multi-dimensional characteristics. Regions can rely on the concept and increase their knowledge-intensive specialization and competitiveness, this is why STPs function as one of the key elements of smart specialization strategies.

In order to create and preserve regional development, a decent strategy is essential to submit for identifying the recent situation and the desired objective and

[1] https://s3platform.jrc.ec.europa.eu/s3-implementation-handbook.

[2] https://s3platform.jrc.ec.europa.eu/-/the-role-of-science-parks-in-smart-specialisation-strategies?inheritRedirect=true&redirect=%2Fscience-parks.

Fig. 2.7 Methodology of regional development creation

make further steps to achieve. According to the RIS3 Guide,[3] the main steps of the regional development methodology is shown in Fig. 2.7.

- During the analysing phase, it is essential to clear what are the main elements fostering regional growth, both considering socio-economic as well as research-innovation field. Defining competitive advantages, weaknesses or bottlenecks of the system is a necessary focus specific area, as it if the initial step to position and compare the regions and economies. It holds the potential of interregional collaboration, utilizing the similarity or complementary of regions, although without a deep analysis there is a risk of excessive fragmentation and loss of synergy potential.
- The participation of stakeholders in design is a ground element of the process. On the other hand, game-changing processes require to increase the competence and to work with other stakeholders as well, in order to improve the knowledge and create a more suitable implementation conditions.
- Having stakeholders engaged to the long-term process, calls for a clear and detailed vision and motivation. The key is the decent communication during the design and process as well, so the undesired situations and misunderstanding can be avoided.
- Synchronizing the RIS3 priorities and the potentials being unfolded during the analysis phase, is a critical step, as the section of potential priorities are those areas where a region have opportunity to emerge. This is the step, where the

[3]https://s3platform.jrc.ec.europa.eu/s3-guide.

activities, projects, actions or technological areas are selected and determined the focus intensity.
- Strategy implementation should be occur through a road map with policy mechanism and instruments. The action plan is the tool of realization the prioritized goals of regions, so in connection to that, it should involve the strategic objectives, time frames and funding sources and budget allocation as well. Pilot projects aimed to test the concept in small scale, before the main investment.
- Monitoring verify the progress of implementation, so it can be the way to be real time and up-to-date, so if it is needed send signal if any further intervention is required. In order to be able to evaluate accurately, the whole strategy should be identified clearly, not just the overall objective, but the sub-goals and tasks as well. For the adequate evaluation requires measurable targets, so we can compare the current and the desired objective. The RIS3 review is carried out by peer regions, which foster the knowledge transfer and learning lessons among regions as regions have direct contact with the potential partners for cooperation. On the other hand, it has to be noted that monitoring phase can not be considered as final step, because a constant demand for innovation, requires the circle to be started again.

2.5 Discussion

The systematic analysis of the success factors of Industry 4.0 readiness models highlighted the importance of the aspect of regional developments. The identification of the external regional success factors initiated the aspiration of building an indicator system for the I4.0+ model, which will be presented in the following chapter.

References

1. Bechtold, J., Lauenstein, C., Kern, A., & Bernhofer, L. (2014). Industry 4.0-the capgemini consulting view. *Capgemnini Consulting, 31*, 32–33.
2. Bertenrath, R., Blum, M., Bleider, M., Millack, A., Schmitt, K., Schmitz, E., et al. (2015). *Industrie 4.0 readiness*. Impuls-Stiftung.
3. Blanchet, M., Rinn, T., Von Thaden, G., & De Thieulloy, G. (2014). Industry 4.0: The new industrial revolution. How Europe will succeed. In *Think Act, Roland Berger strategy consultants GmbH* .
4. Commissione Europea (2014). For a European industrial renaissance. *COM (2014), 14*(2), 1–23.
5. Ettlinger, N. (2017). Open innovation and its discontents. *Geoforum, 80*, 61–71.
6. European Commission (2019). *Eu budget for the future*.
7. Foidl, H., & Felderer, M. (2015). Research challenges of industry 4.0 for quality management. In *International Conference on Enterprise Resource Planning Systems* (pp. 121–137). Berlin: Springer.
8. Gaofeng, Y. (2019). Cross-border collaboration strategies in academic entrepreneurship of new r&d institutions: Insights from explorative case studies in china. *Science, Technology and Society, 24*(2), 288–315.

9. Geissbauer, R., Vedso, J., & Schrauf, S. (2016). *Industry 4.0: Building the digital enterprise*. Retrieved from PwC Website: https://www.pwc.com/gx/en/industries/industries-4.0/landing-page/industry-4.0-building-your-digital-enterprise-april-2016.pdf
10. González Fernández, S., Kubus, R., & Mascareñas Pérez-Iñigo, J. (2019). Innovation ecosystems in the eu: Policy evolution and horizon Europe proposal case study (the actors' perspective). *Sustainability, 11*(17), 4735.
11. Grillitsch, M., Rekers, J. V., & Tödtling, F. (2019). When drivers of clusters shift scale from local towards global: What remains for regional innovation policy? *Geoforum, 102*, 57–68.
12. He, D., Zheng, M., Cheng, W., Lau, Y.-y., & Yin, Q. (2019). Interaction between higher education outputs and industrial structure evolution: Evidence from hubei province, china. *Sustainability, 11*(10), 2923 (2019).
13. Imran, F., & Kantola, J. (2018). Review of industry 4.0 in the light of sociotechnical system theory and competence-based view: A future research agenda for the evolute approach. In *International Conference on Applied Human Factors and Ergonomics* (pp. 118–128). Berlin: Springer.
14. Jagannathan, S., Ra, S., & Maclean, R. (2019). Dominant recent trends impacting on jobs and labor markets-an overview. *International Journal of Training Research, 17*(supl), 1–11.
15. Joint Research Centre (2019). *The cultural and creative cities monitor*. Publications Office of the European Union.
16. Krause, W., Schutte, C., & Du Preez, N. (2012). Open innovation in South African small and medium-sized enterprises. In *CIE42 Conference Proceedings, Cape Town*.
17. Manda, M. I., & Dhaou, S. B. (2019). Responding to the challenges and opportunities in the 4th industrial revolution in developing countries. In *Proceedings of the 12th International Conference on Theory and Practice of Electronic Governance* (pp. 244–253). New York: ACM.
18. Matulova, P., Maresova, P., Tareq, M. A., & Kuča, K. (2018). Open innovation session as a tool supporting innovativeness in strategies for high-tech companies in the Czech republic. *Economies, 6*(4), 69.
19. Menon, K., Kärkkäinen, H., Wuest, T., & Gupta, J. P. (2019). Industrial internet platforms: A conceptual evaluation from a product lifecycle management perspective. *Proceedings of the Institution of Mechanical Engineers, Part B: Journal of Engineering Manufacture, 233*(5), 1390–1401.
20. Merkelbach, I., Hollanders, H., & Es-Sadki, N. (2019). *European innovation scoreboard 2019*.
21. Miszlivetz, F., & Márkus, E. (2013). A kraft-index–kreatív városok–fenntartható vidék (the kraft index: Creative cities–sustainable regions). *Vezetéstudomány-Budapest Management Review, 44*(9), 2–21.
22. Nagy, J. (2019). Az ipar 4.0 fogalma és kritikus kérdései–vállalati interjúk alapján. *Vezetéstudomány-Budapest Management Review, 50*(1), 14–26.
23. Nick, G., & Pongrácz, F. (2016). How to measure industry 4.0 readiness of cities. *International Scientific Journal Industry, 4*(2), 64–68.
24. Nowacki, C., & Monk, A. (2020). Ambidexterity in government: The influence of different types of legitimacy on innovation. *Research Policy, 49*(1), 103840 (2020).
25. Paola Annoni, L. D. (2019). Regional competitiveness index 2019. In *European commission, joint research centre*.
26. Richardson, L., & Bissell, D. (2017). Geographies of digital skill. *Geoforum, 99*, 278–286.
27. Schumacher, A., Erol, S., & Sihn, W. (2016). A maturity model for assessing industry 4.0 readiness and maturity of manufacturing enterprises. *Procedia Cirp, 52*, 161–166.
28. Schumacher, A., Nemeth, T., & Sihn, W. (2019). Roadmapping towards industrial digitalization based on an industry 4.0 maturity model for manufacturing enterprises. *Procedia CIRP, 79*, 409–414.
29. Sonn, J. W., Hess, M., & Wang, H. (2019). Spaces for creativity? Skills and deskilling in cultural and high-tech industries. *Geoforum, 99*, 223–226.
30. Stromquist, N. P. (2019). World development report 2019: The changing nature of work. *International Review of Education, 65*, 321–329.

31. Temple, A. F., Díaz Gamarra, M. A., & Sánchez Zambrano, M. E. (2019). Triple collaboration for innovation and sustainability: A case study of a manufacturing enterprise. *The International Journal of Sustainability Policy and Practice, 15*(1), 51–65.
32. Trotta, D., & Garengo, P. (2019). Assessing industry 4.0 maturity: An essential scale for SMEs. In *2019 8th International Conference on Industrial Technology and Management (ICITM)* (pp. 69–74). Piscataway: IEEE.
33. Tvenge, N., & Martinsen, K. (2018). Integration of digital learning in industry 4.0. *Procedia Manufacturing, 23*, 261–266.
34. Viharos, Z. J., Soós, S., Nick, G. A., Várgedő, T., & Beregi, R. J. (2017). Non-comparative, industry 4.0 readiness evaluation for manufacturing enterprises. In *15th IMEKO TC10 Workshop on Technical Diagnostics. Technical Diagnostics in Cyber-Physical Era, Budapest.*
35. Wang, S., Wan, J., Li, D., & Zhang, C. (2016). Implementing smart factory of industrie 4.0: An outlook. *International Journal of Distributed Sensor Networks, 12*(1), 3159805.
36. World Economic Forum (2016). The future of jobs: Employment, skills and workforce strategy for the fourth industrial revolution. In *Global Challenge Insight Report, World Economic Forum, Geneva.*
37. World Economic Forum. *The future of jobs report 2018*. World Economic Forum, Geneva.
38. Zmiyak, S. S., Ugnich, E. A., & Taranov, P. M. (2020). Development of a regional innovation ecosystem: The role of a pillar university. In *Growth poles of the global economy: Emergence, changes and future perspectives* (pp. 567–576). Berlin: Springer.

Chapter 3
Measures of Regional Industry 4.0 + Readiness

3.1 Determination of the Utilized Data Sources

As a detailed and corroborated data set is sought, we utilise three types of data sources. Firstly, in Sect. 3.1.1, the sources of the studied open government statistical data is shown. Secondly, in Sect. 3.1.2, we reveal other sources used as regional reports or other open data portals concerning different areas. Finally, in Sect. 3.1.3, The GDELT Project is interpreted as a source for measuring the number of media appearances and its tone with regard to I4.0-related topics applied to the NUTS 2 regional level.

3.1.1 Statistical Data Sources

In order to be able to see through the current situation of regions, regional statistical databases were used as a source of single indicators. The target GEO level is the NUTS2 regional level, so concerning this Eurostat Regional statistics according to the NUTS classification were used [5].[1]

To narrow down the statistical database, Table 3.1 shows the exact "location" of the examined indicators. The temporal and spatial references are also indicated. On the time horizon, at least 4 years of coverage is present. According to the spatial horizon, the NUTS 2 regional level is the sole focus.

[1] https://ec.europa.eu/eurostat/data/database.

J. Abonyi et al., *Are Regions Prepared for Industry 4.0?*, SpringerBriefs in Entrepreneurship and Innovation, https://doi.org/10.1007/978-3-030-53103-4_3

Table 3.1 Analysed statistical indicators to measure I4.0 activities

Indicator	Years	NUTS class	Ref.
Population on 1 January by age, sex and NUTS 2 region (demo_r_d2jan)	2014–2018	NUTS 2	[12]
Population aged 25–64 by educational attainment level, sex and NUTS 2 regions (%) (edat_lfse_04)	2014–2018	NUTS 2	[10]
Population aged 30–34 by educational attainment level, sex and NUTS 2 regions (%) (edat_lfse_12)	2014–2018	NUTS 2	[11]
Employment rates of young people not in education and training by sex, educational attainment level, years since completion of highest level of education and NUTS 2 regions (edat_lfse_33)	2014–2018	NUTS 2	[7]
Human Resources in Science and Technology (HRST) by category and NUTS 2 regions (hrst_st_rcat)	2014–2018	NUTS 2	[8]
Employment in technology and knowledge-intensive sectors by NUTS 2 regions and sex (from 2008 onwards, NACE Rev. 2) (htec_emp_reg2)	2014–2018	NUTS 2	[6]
Intramural R&D expenditure (GERD) by sectors of performance and NUTS 2 regions (rd_e_gerdreg)	2012–2016	NUTS 2	[9]
Total R&D personnel and researchers by sectors of performance, sex and NUTS 2 regions (rd_p_persreg)	2012–2016	NUTS 2	[13]

3.1.2 Alternative Metrics

Beyond statistical data sources, we used reports and other open data portals in order to broaden the selection of data and make our concept more specific. In this regard, altmetrics stands for being beyond traditional or "simple", but also paying attention to the availability of sources.

We used up-to-date reports in the field of regional development and innovation. These reports created indicator systems which can rank regions or cities according to field of research.

Table 3.2 was made to demonstrate these "other data sources", which have been broadened by the following descriptions of sources:

1. The Regional Innovation Scoreboard (RIS) [18][2] 2019 was published by the European Commission. It "provides a comparative assessment of the performance of innovation systems across 238 regions of 23 EU Member States, Norway, Serbia, and Switzerland.". This report is applicable to investors or companies who want to invest, as they can assess and compare regions in terms of innovation capability.

[2]https://ec.europa.eu/growth/industry/innovation/facts-figures/regional_en.

Table 3.2 Analysed reports and open data portals as a sources of data

Source	Type	Examined indicator/data	Time horizon	Spatial horizon
Regional Innovation Scoreboard (RIS)	Report	Innovative SMEs collaborating with others as a percentage of SMEs	NUTS 1 and 2 for different countries for CIS 2008, CIS 2010, CIS 2012, CIS 2014, CIS 2016	NUTS 1 and 2 for different countries for CIS 2008, CIS 2010, CIS 2012, CIS 2014, CIS 2016
Regional Competitiveness Index (RCI)	Report	Knowledge workers (% of total employment)	Average 2015–2017	NUTS 2
Cultural and Creative Cities (C3)	Report	Average appearances in university rankings	2018	City
ETER	Open data portal	Graduates in IT, Engineering or Mathematics (BSc, MSc, PhD)	2008–2016	NUTS 2
Erasmus	Open data portal	Number of students participating in mobility programmes	2008–2013	NUTS 2
MA-Graph	Open data portal	Publications by categories	2008–2018	NUTS 2
GRID	Open data portal	Distribution of institutions by categories	–	NUTS 2
USPTO	Open data portal	I4.0-related patent applications at the NUTS 2 level	2008–2018	NUTS 2
CORDIS	Open data portal	Collaboration between organizations under Horizon 2020	2014–2020	NUTS 2

2. The Regional Competitiveness Index (RCI) [17][3] 2019 was "published some 10 years after the global financial crisis". It aims to measure the competitive capability of regions and predict the future of our economy.
3. Cultural and Creative Cities (C3) [2][4] is a "tool designed to monitor and benchmark the performance of Cultural and Creative Cities in Europe". It makes it possible to monitor cities over time by stakeholders, which can also be advantageous in decision-making.
4. ETER (European Tertiary Education Register) [4][5] is an online platform, which stores information about European Higher Education Institutes. By the use of this platform, we are able to gain information about the number of students, graduates, international doctorates, staff, fields of education, income and expenditure as well as descriptive information on their characteristics.
5. The Erasmus+ Program [3],[6] is a Study Mobility Program, which combines seven EU education, training and youth programs. It is an integral part of the Lifelong Learning Programme (LLP).

   It was our intention to measure the number of students participating in a study mobility program (both those leaving and arriving in a given region). However, to be more specific, we chose two main fields of education, which are related to I4.0, namely (1) Science, Mathematics and Computing and (2) Engineering, Manufacturing and Construction.
6. The Microsoft Academic Graph (MA Graph) [16][7] was established in 2015 and since then it has been updated on weekly basis. This platform gathers "scientific publication records, citation relationships between those publications, as well as authors, institutions, journals, conferences, and fields of study". As a result, the research activity can be measured according to the field of publication, year of publication or the issuing institution.
7. The Global Research Identifier Database (GRID) [14][8] is an online data portal, which aims to foster interoperability and data exchange among the scientific community. It provides beneficial information about institutions e.g. geographic features, location, or the institution profile. On the other hand, it is connected with external links, so the facilities of usage are broadened. It can be a source to determine the density of institutions as "proxy" indicators, for example, the density of companies which can lead up the conclusion about the job opportunities in cities/regions/countries. (It should be noted that not all institutions are registered.)

---

[3] https://ec.europa.eu/regional_policy/en/information/publications/working-papers/2019/the-european-regional-competitiveness-index-2019.

[4] https://ec.europa.eu/jrc/en/publication/eur-scientific-and-technical-research-reports/cultural-and-creative-cities-monitor-2019-edition.

[5] https://eter-project.com/#/home.

[6] https://acro.ceu.edu/erasmus-mobility-program.

[7] https://www.microsoft.com/en-us/research/project/microsoft-academic-graph/.

[8] https://www.grid.ac/.

8. United States Patent and Trademark Office (USPTO) [20][9] is an American online platform that collects patent applications from U.S. states/territories as well as foreign countries and regions where at least one utility patent originated. This source makes it possible to monitor regional (technical) development by identifying the patent applications by regions.
9. CORDIS [1][10] is a database supported by Horizon 2020 (2014–2020). This dataset includes both projects and organizations funded under the Horizon 2020 framework.

   Thanks to the Horizon 2020 Collaboration Network, both the exact location of organizations as well as the H2020 hot-spots can be seen. Furthermore, these organizations have been counted and which ones collaborated with each other in H2020 research and innovation projects indicated.

   It highly reflects knowledge transfer from one region to another. We can step out from the local organization to the glocal "collaboration map" into the global perspective of data exchange.

3.1.3 Indicator Based on Number of News Related to Industry 4.0

The GDELT Project [19][11] is one of the largest open databases, which makes it possible to overcome the Spatio-temporal boundaries. It forms the connections between people, organizations, locations, themes, counts, images and emotions worldwide.

We attempt to utilize the potential of this database determine the opinion of the world about Industry 4.0-related topics and news by accumulating the number of I4.0-related news by NUTS 2 regions.

In order to precisely examine the appearance of I4.0-related news, four main topics, namely innovation, automation, research and development and SMEs, were considered. In this regard, Fig. 3.1, shows the search words and areas examined.

[9] https://patents.reedtech.com/patent-products.php.

[10] https://cordis.europa.eu/datalab/datalab.php?cfg=organizations&menu=collaboration#.

[11] https://www.gdeltproject.org/.

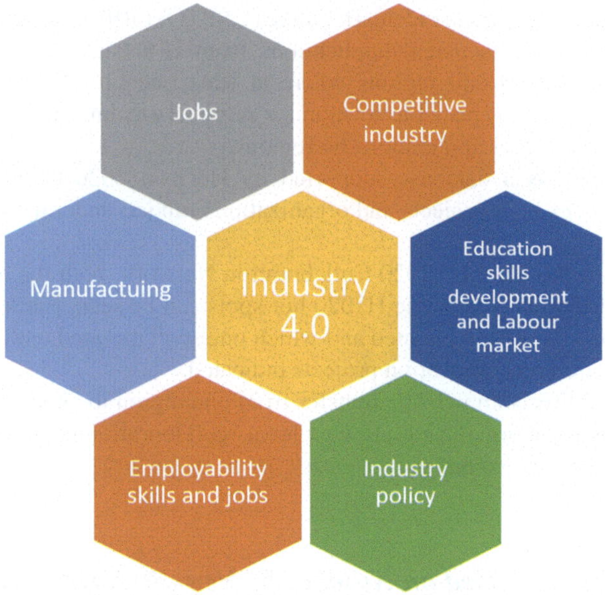

Fig. 3.1 Search words for GDELT, in order to observe the appearance of Industry 4.0-related media appearances

3.2 Association of Indicators and Variables

In this section, we seek to describe the selected indicators based on the aforementioned data sources. In the light of this, we created indicator groups which are characterized to foster regional development.

These five topics are shown in Fig. 3.2. They are all linked to each other and amplify their effect in terms of both social and economic aspects.

Higher education is like a driving force of knowledge creation, which provides a well-educated workforce for the labour market, moreover, in this sector, a chance to support the innovative actors, like research institutions is given. The innovative capability of a region can redound the ability to apply technological developments of the present. On the other hand, investment is essential to promote knowledge transfer, however, without financial support, projects may not be implemented in SMEs or institutions. These sectors aim to enhance the competitiveness and development of a region and, therefore, improve the quality of life.

In the following, sections are categorized by the indicator groups interpreted above. In Sect. 3.2.1, we are going to highlight the importance of higher education and lifelong learning, corroborate the displayed indicators. In Sect. 3.2.2, the

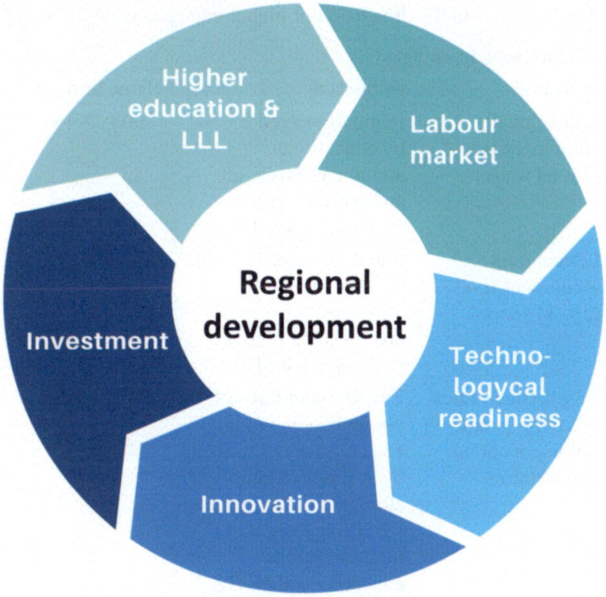

Fig. 3.2 Regional development related indicator groups

labour market and its I4.0-related indicators are interpreted. Activities that foster innovation and variables are shown in Sect. 3.2.3. On the other hand, the relevance of investments cannot be neglected, as this is one of the major driving forces of development, so in Sect. 3.2.4, we demonstrate indicators related to that. Finally, in Sect. 3.2.5, technological readiness related variables are shown.

3.2.1 The Pillar of Higher Education

Human capital is undoubtedly a key factor in competitiveness and growth. As has already been highlighted, education and university are the keys to knowledge and one of the driving forces of innovation. The high proportion of the workforce which is poorly educated can have an adverse effect on the economy. The following figures visualize the regions in terms of educational level, i.e. which ones are more "ready" and which are backward.

In the name of higher education and lifelong learning, we list indicators, which are relevant in the field and able to indicate the intensity of one of the "driving forces". These are shown in Table 3.3:

Table 3.3 Analysed indicators in the dimension of higher education and lifelong learning

Higher education and lifelong learning				
Source	Indicator	Definition	Time horizon	Spatial horizon
Eurostat	Educational attainment level (25–64 years)	Population aged 25–64 by educational attainment level, sex and NUTS 2 regions (%) (edat_lfse_04)	2008–2018	NUTS 2
	Educational attainment level (30–34 years)	Population aged 30–34 by educational attainment level, sex and NUTS 2 regions (%) (edat_lfse_12)	2008–2018	NUTS 2
	Employment rates of young people not in education and training	Employment rates of young people not in education and training by sex, educational attainment level, years since completion of highest level of education and NUTS 2 regions (edat_lfse_33)	2008–2018	NUTS 2
Cultural and Creative Cities (C3)	Average appearances in university rankings	Average number of appearances of universities in four different university rankings: QS, Shanghai, Leiden and Times	2018	City
ETER	Graduates in IT, Engineering or Mathematics (BSc, MSc, PhD)	Number of graduates in IT, Engineering or Mathematics. (BSc, MSc, PhD)	2008–2016	NUTS 2
Erasmus	Number of students participating in mobility programmes	Number of student s going to/returning from studying abroad (by mobility programme) in the relevant field	2008–2013	NUTS 2
GRID	Distribution of educational institutions	Number of educational institutions	–	NUTS 2

1. Educational attainment level (25–64 years) reflects the percentage of the population that falls into different levels of educational attainment (Upper secondary, post-secondary non-tertiary and tertiary education (levels 3–8), Upper secondary and post-secondary non-tertiary education (levels 3 and 4) and Tertiary education (levels 5–8)). Its density is shown in Fig. 3.3.

   This indicator can be connected to lifelong learning activities thanks to the age-group preference and educational level ranking. It can be used as a basis for identifying the regional "aspiration" to keep up with the continually changing environment and demand for skills. On the other hand, from the level of educational attainment it is also clear that capital cities have a pulling effect on the surroundings as "invite" knowledge to the region.

2. Educational attainment level (30–34 years) offers a narrowed perspective of the aforementioned indicator as the age group is only between 30 and 34 years. It measures the percentage of attainment of the population in terms of educational level.
3. Employment rate of young people not in education and training (15–34 years) is an indicator which aims to measure the gap between when young people finish education and entered the labour market. It can be separated according to duration as well as educational level to clarify which segment is the most active as is visible in Fig. 3.4.
4. The average appearance the in university rankings is aimed to indicate institutions which are the most preferred. It is worth observing how this ranking effects the study mobility programs and the pull of knowledge into regions from their surroundings.
5. The number of students participating in study mobility programs shows the additional number of students leaving and arriving in the given region. As previously mentioned a correlation exists between the tempting effect of universities and the mobility of students. It must be highlighted that we only observe the mobility of students in two fields, namely Science, Mathematics and Computing, and Engineering, Manufacturing and Construction.
6. Graduates in I4.0-related fields, such as IT, Engineering and Natural Sciences can be one of the major forces of the I4.0-related higher education pillar. Firstly, this indicator shows which regions provide educational training in the field and make it possible to prepare and equip students with the skills demanded in the concept of I4.0. On the other hand, the number of graduates in the field reflects the size of the supply on the labour market in the related fields.
7. The density of educational institutions within a region is also a key factor, as these institutions are responsible for generating knowledge and providing the highly skilled workforce of the future. On the other hand, they have an influence on innovation capability as well. The number of institutions per region can be related to the educational attainment level (the size and population of a region is also important).

3.2.2 *Labour Market*

There is a strong relationship between the labour market and education, as the work force reflects the number of people educated in a particular field. Of course, the demand of the labour market must also be taken into consideration.

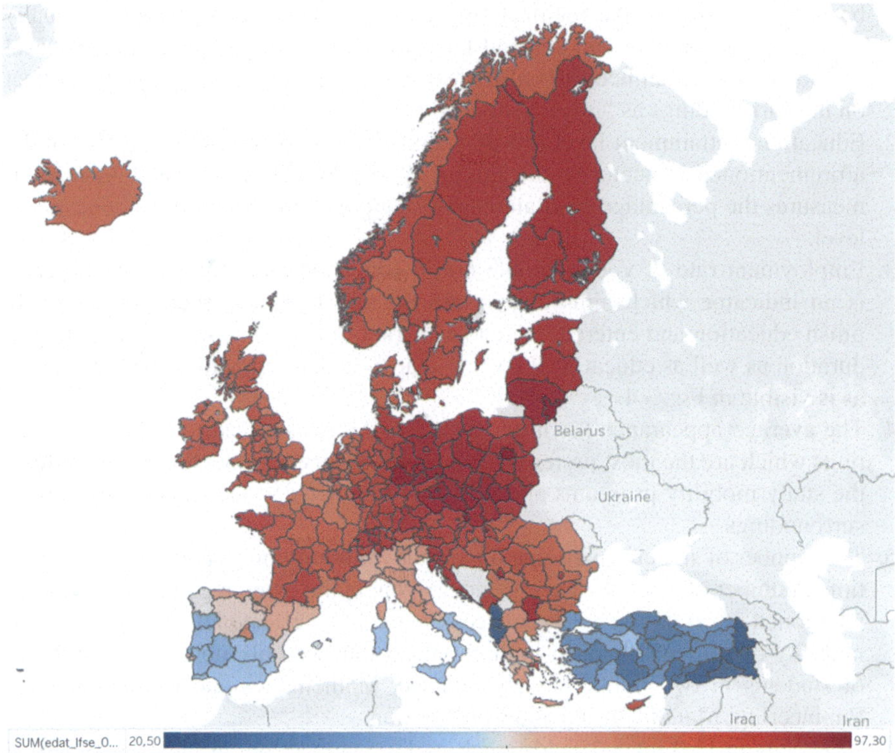

Fig. 3.3 The educational attainment level in upper secondary, post-secondary non-tertiary and tertiary education between 25 and 64 years of age (2018)

Nowadays, in the age of Conscious Industrialization, job contents have changed. On the other hand, "economic, industrial and labour market policies that are responsive and can better prepare industry, citizens, and government for the opportunities brought by the 4th industrial revolution" [15]. In terms of digitalization and robotization, a growing need exists for high-tech and knowledge-intensive services. In order to continually keep up with the demand, education systems are required to operate efficiently and maintain high standards.

According to this pillar, we listed indicators in Table 3.4, which play a significant role in determining the readiness of the labour market.

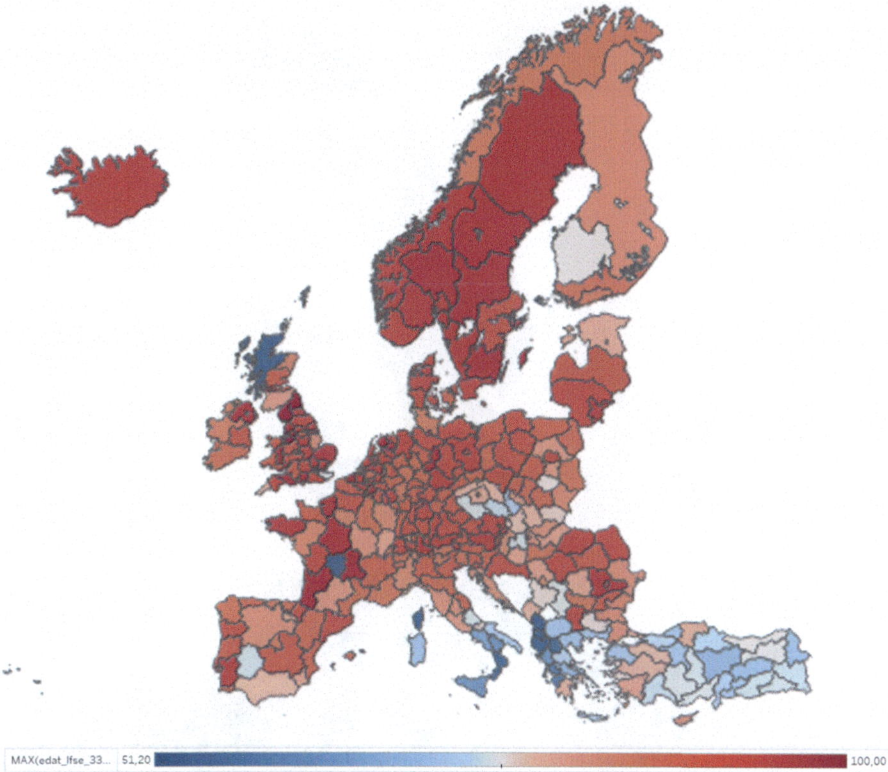

Fig. 3.4 Employment rates of young people not in education and training with the highest level of education (Upper secondary, post-secondary non-tertiary and tertiary education) (2018)

Table 3.4 Analysed indicators in the dimension of Labour market

Labour market				
Source	Indicator	Definition	Time horizon	NUTS
Eurostat	Employment in the technology and knowledge-intensive sectors	Employment in technology and knowledge-intensive sectors by NUTS 2 regions and sex (from 2008 onwards, NACE Rev. 2) (htec_emp_reg2)	2008–2018	NUTS 2
GDELT	Distribution of I4.0-related media appearance	Number of articles related to I4.0 in the media by NUTS 2 regions	2018	NUTS 2
GRID	Density of institutions by categories	Number of companies in NUTS 2 regional level	–	City

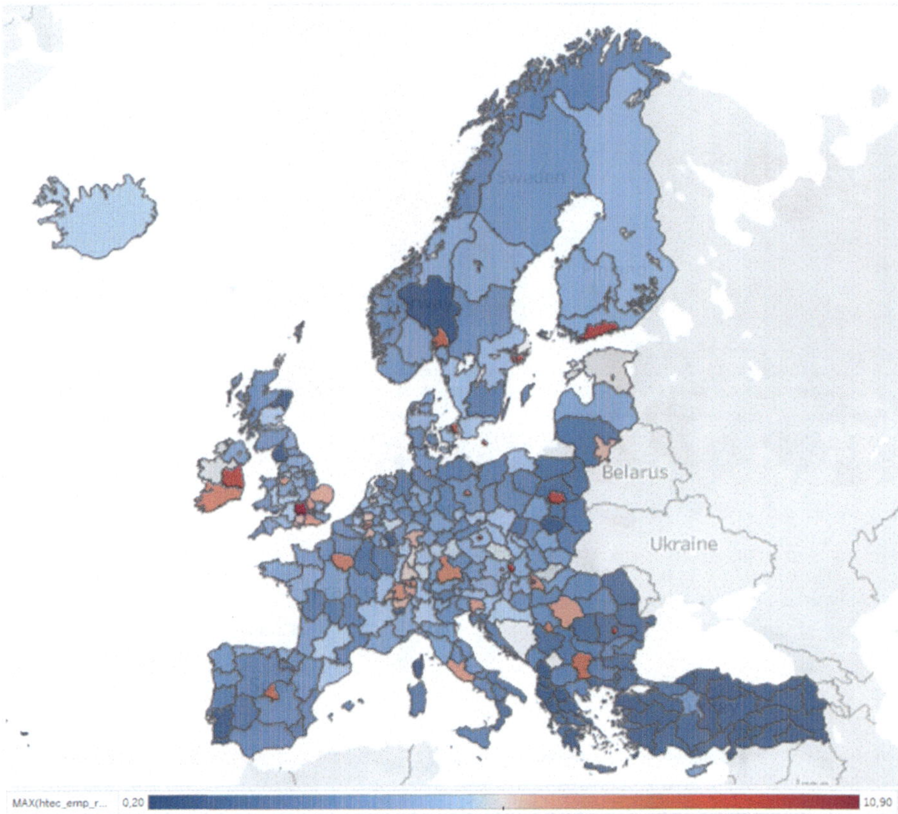

Fig. 3.5 Employment in the high-technology sectors (high-technology manufacturing and knowledge-intensive high-technology services) (2018)

1. Employment in the technology and knowledge-intensive sectors reflects the percentage of employment in the chosen[12] economic activities related to I4.0. Its distribution is shown in Fig. 3.5.

   This can be used to identify the intensity of regional labour market in I4.0-related economic activities, for example as a "proxy" to approximate technological readiness. It can be paired with the higher education pillar, more likely with the number of graduates in the relevant field, and can indicate both the supply and demand of the market.

[12]High-technology sectors (high-technology manufacturing and knowledge-intensive high-technology services), Manufacturing, High and medium high-technology manufacturing, Medium high-technology manufacturing, High-technology manufacturing, Low and medium low-technology manufacturing, Medium low-technology manufacturing, Low-technology manufacturing, Total knowledge-intensive services, Knowledge-intensive high-technology services, Professional, scientific and technical activities, Education.

2. The distribution of companies within a region indicates the available employment opportunities, as well as the possibility for open innovation and collaboration with external parties. In correlation with the aforementioned indicator, it can be identified how the number of companies is related to the percentage of people working in the technology and knowledge-intensive sector.
3. The distribution of I4.0-related media appearance is a creative way of measuring how many regions deal with the issues and/or results of the relevant field (Innovation, automation, research and development as well as SMEs). These have been identified by the search words mentioned in Fig. 3.1.

3.2.3 Innovation Activities

The innovation pillar is a critical component of the I4.0 concept, as the conscious formation of the present and future would benefit from improvements to foster innovation activities. Not only R&D factor but also academic and governmental support is essential. In the field of regional readiness, we aimed to sought those indicators which can reflect on the innovation capability of the given region. These are listed in Table 3.5.

1. Human Resources in Science and Technology (HRST) has been categorised,[13] and these categories all support the innovation capability of a region. It measures these values in NUTS 2 regions either as a percentage of the total population or one thousand people as is highlighted in Fig. 3.6.

   This indicator, given its availability, makes it possible for individuals to foresee which regions are the most advanced in the field of employment of science and technology or which ones need to keep up with the others. It is worth mentioning how this indicator can correlate with graduates in the relevant field and also with the number of publications and patent applications.
2. The collaboration of innovative SMEs measures the percentage of SMEs involved in innovative co-operation with others. It is indicative of knowledge and information flow between SMEs and other institutions.
3. CORDIS—Collaboration between organizations in the context of H2020 research and innovation projects. There are several opportunities to use this indicator, as it reflects both the method of knowledge transfer, as well as the visualization of spatial collaborations. We can identify the hot spots to determine which regions are most likely to implement open innovation.

[13] Persons with tertiary education (ISCED) and/or employed in science and technology, Persons with tertiary education (ISCED), Persons employed in science and technology, Persons with tertiary education (ISCED) and employed in science and technology, and Scientists and engineers.

Table 3.5 Analysed indicators in the dimension of innovation activities

Innovation activities				
Source	Indicator	Definition	Time horizon	Spatial horizon
Eurostat	Human Resources in Science and Technology	HRST by category and NUTS 2 regions (hrst_st_rcat)	2008–2018	NUTS 2
Regional Innovation Scoreboard (RIS)	Innovative SMEs collaborating with others as a percentage of SMEs	This indicator measures the degree to which SMEs are involved in innovation co-operation. The indicator measures the flow of knowledge between public research institutions and firms, and between firms and other firms	NUTS 1 and 2 for different countries	NUTS 1 and 2 for different countries
Eurostat	Employment in the technology and knowledge-intensive sectors	Employment in the technology and knowledge-intensive sectors by NUTS 2 regions and sex (from 2008 onwards, NACE Rev. 2) (htec_emp_reg2)	2008–2018	NUTS 2
USPTO	Patents	Number of patent applications in the relevant field by regions	2008–2018	NUTS 2
CORDIS	Collaboration intensity	Cooperation in the name of the H2020 project between regions	2014–2020	NUTS 2
MA-Graph	Publications by categories	Number of publications (at least two I4.0-related topic included)	2008–2018	NUTS 2

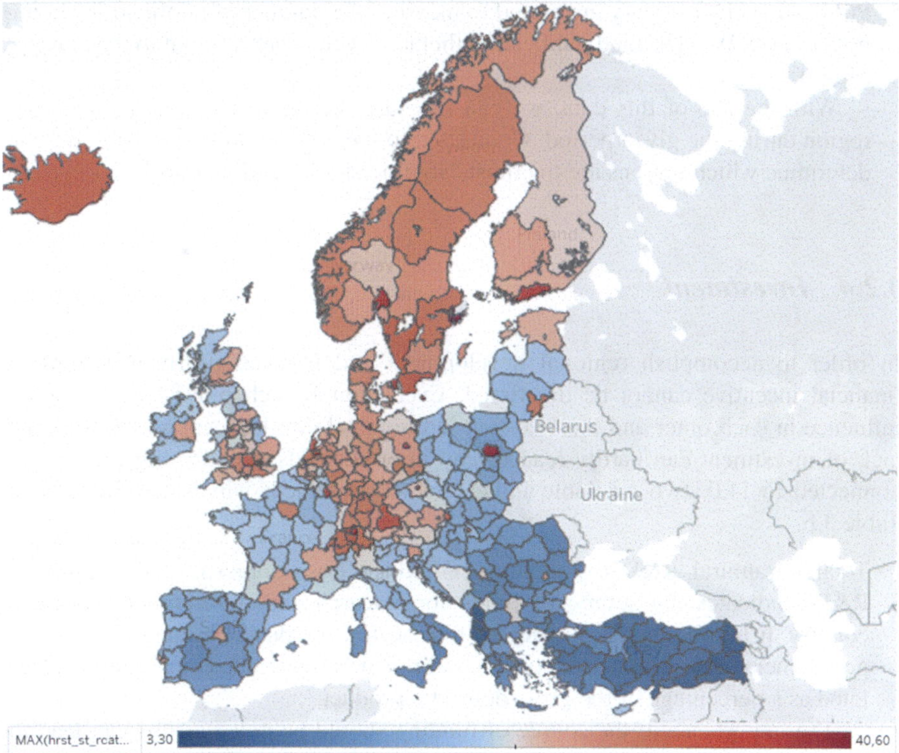

Fig. 3.6 Human Resources in Science and Technology: employment in science and technology as a percentage of the total population (2018)

4. In terms of patent applications, we targeted the major patent groups[14] connected to I4.0. By using this indicator, it is possible determine the density of patent applications by calculating the number of I4.0-related patent applications in the given NUTS 2 region.

   It reflects the ability and willingness of a region to adapt new ideas and technological developments.

[14] Additive manufacturing technology, Nanotechnology, Machines or engines in general; Engine plants in general; Steam engines, Controlling; Regulating, Computing; Calculating, Counting, Signaling, Information and communication technology (ICT) specially adapted for specific application fields.

5. Publications by category are aimed to measure the number of publications in the field of I4.0. We classified publication themes[15] which are relevant to the concept of I4.0.

   With the use of this data, we can measure the number of publications per region during the given period. Connected to the collaboration intensity, we can determine which regions are the most "significant I4.0 collaborators".

3.2.4 *Investment*

In order to accomplish regional development and innovation-driven actions, a financial incentive cannot be dismissed. Even though each pillar have a capital influence in each other and the I4.0-focused regional development as a whole, the lack of investment can hardly lead to any improvements. Concerning investment connected to I4.0, two available indicators were studied, which can be seen in Table 3.6.

1. Total intramural R&D expenditure (GERD—Gross domestic expenditure on R&D) indicates the source of funds for research and development within a country. It highlights the potency of four sector, the business enterprise sector, government sector, higher education and private non-profit sector, and is calculated as a percentage of the gross domestic product.

   The importance of the source of funding should be noted as this can lead to improvement.

   This indicator can be used to determine the density of the financial support of R&D of regions by sectors. This indicator can be connected to all pillar concerning the sectors and their impact on each other.

Table 3.6 Analysed indicators in the dimension of investment

Investment				
Source	Indicator	Definition	Time horizon	NUTS
Eurostat	Total intramural R&D expenditure	Intramural R&D expenditure (GERD) by sectors of performance and NUTS 2 regions (rd_e_gerdreg)	2008–2016	NUTS 2
Eurostat	Total R&D personnel and researchers	Total R&D personnel and researchers by sectors of performance, sex and NUTS 2 regions (rd_p_persreg)	2008–2016	NUTS 2

[15]Industrial engineering, Operations management, Process engineering, Transport engineering, Operations research, Simulation, Knowledge management, Control theory, Telecommunications, Mechanical engineering, Computer engineering, Software engineering, Manufacturing engineering, Machine learning, Data mining, Mathematical optimization, Control engineering, Regional science, Embedded system, Artificial intelligence, Process management, Reliability engineering, Systems engineering, Management science, Data science.

2. The indicator "Total R&D personnel and researchers" is calculated as either the percentage of total employment or by a headcount according to our definition. It consists of individuals employed in research and development, moreover, takes into consideration the direct services as well as researchers employed in the public or private sectors as academia. Here we distinguish also four sectors, namely business, government, higher education and private sector. Their densities are visualized in Fig. 3.7.

   This indicator makes it possible to identify the knowledge workers in each sector who are the driving force of knowledge and innovation and facilitate improvement in the creative environment.

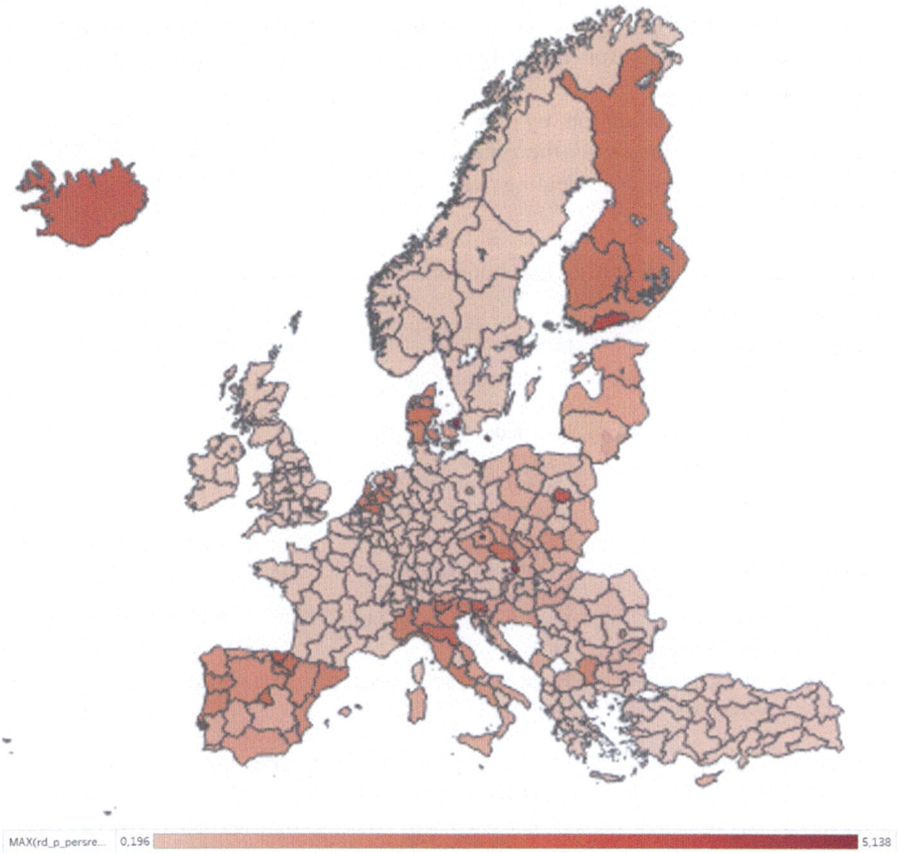

Fig. 3.7 Regional density of total R&D personnel and researchers as a percentage of total employment (2016)

3.2.5 Technological Readiness

It is a challenging task to identify regional technological readiness, SMEs and technical equipment of businesses alone cannot be relied on, the regional potential to create a decent environment for adapting and utilize emerging technologies is also important. In regard with the technological readiness pillar of regional Industry 4.0 model, the following indicators are listed in Table 3.7.

1. Employment in the technology and knowledge-intensive sectors, as already mentioned in the labour market pillar, is strongly related to technology as well as the labour market. In this view, we can determine the capability of employment to adapt to new technologies, e.g. the already existing jobs in this field.
2. The number of graduates in I4.0-related fields in terms of those from IT, Engineering or Mathematics. This does exhibit a fostering effect from a technological point of view as graduates can be considered to be “knowledge transfers” that provide a basis for innovation and improvement in the technological environment.
3. The indicator “Publication by categories”[16] is also relevant in the field of technological readiness, as the output of publications in the relevant field can indicate that regions are dealing with up-to-date technologies and innovative

Table 3.7 Analysed indicators in the dimension of technological readiness

Technological readiness				
Source	Indicator	Definition	Time horizon	Spatial horizon
Eurostat	Employment in the technology and knowledge-intensive sector	Employment in the technology and knowledge-intensive sectors by NUTS 2 regions and sex (from 2008 onwards, NACE Rev. 2) (htec_emp_reg2)	2008–2018	NUTS 2
ETER	Graduates in IT, Engineering or Mathematics (BSc, MSc, PhD)	Number of graduates in IT, Engineering or Mathematics. (BSc, MSc, PhD)	2008–2013	NUTS 2
MA-Graph	Publications by categories	Number of publications (at least two I4.0—related topic included)	2008–2018	NUTS 2
USPTO	Patents	Number of patent applications in the relevant field by regions	2008–2018	NUTS 2

[16] Industrial engineering, Operations management, Process engineering, Transport engineering, Operations research, Simulation, Knowledge management, Control theory, Telecommunications, Mechanical engineering, Computer engineering, Software engineering, Manufacturing engineering, Machine learning, Data mining, Mathematical optimization, Control engineering, Regional science, Embedded system, Artificial intelligence, Process management, Reliability engineering, Systems engineering, Management science, Data science.

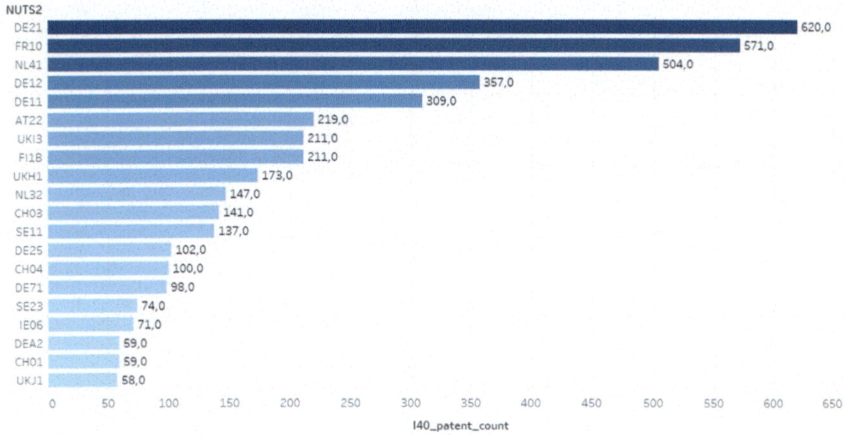

Fig. 3.8 Top 20 NUTS 2 regions according to the number of I4.0-related patent applications

actions. Similarly, software engineering, simulation or machine learning, data mining, etc. can reveal the aspiration of a region to take innovation to the next level.

4. The density of patent applications points towards the measurement of technological readiness by identifying the patent groups[17] and connecting with the given region. It does reflect the innovation actions in the field. The top 20 regions can be seen according to the number of patent applications in Fig. 3.8.

3.3 Indicator Table Measuring Regional I4.0 Readiness

In this section, the chosen indicators will be interpreted and the main objectives highlighted.

As has already been emphasized, we seek for the NUTS 2 spatial coverage, so indicators were chosen and generated in the light of this fact. By this coverage, the "glocal" aspect of I4.0 readiness can be observed. Neither can the temporal coverage be dismissed as the I4.0 concept has been discussed since 2012, data availability from 2012 onwards.

As was discussed in Sect. 3.1.2, we used data portals and reports as databases which are open and available. This facilitates monitoring, as our goal is to create a complex and coherent indicator system which measures regional readiness.

Tables 3.8 and 3.9 reflect on the statements above, show the chosen indicators categorised and indicate the spatial and temporal horizons and their availability.

---

[17] Additive manufacturing technology, Nanotechnology, Machines or engines in general; Engine plants in general; Steam engines, Controlling; Regulating, Computing; Calculating, Counting, Signaling, Information and communication technology (ICT) specially adapted for specific application fields.

Table 3.8 Analysed indicators grouped according to the field supported by regional development (Higher education and Labour market) (I-Included, D-Discarded)

Source	Indicator	Definition	Time horizon	Spatial horizon	Used
Higher Education and Lifelong Learning					
Eurostat	Educational attainment level (25–64 years)	Population aged 25–64 by educational attainment level, sex and NUTS 2 regions (%) (edat_lfse_04)	2008–2018	NUTS 2	I
	Educational attainment level (30–34 years)	Population aged 30–34 by educational attainment level, sex and NUTS 2 regions (%) (edat_lfse_12)	2008–2018	NUTS 2	I
	Employment rates of young people not in education and training	Employment rates of young people not in education and training by sex, educational attainment level, years since completion of highest level of education and NUTS 2 regions (edat_lfse_33)	2008–2018	NUTS 2	I
Cultural and Creative Cities (C3)	Average number of appearances in university rankings	Average number of appearances of universities in four different university rankings: QS, Shanghai, Leiden and Times	2018	NUTS 2	D

Eter	Graduates in IT, Engineering or Mathematics (BSc, MSc, PhD)	Number of people graduates in IT, Engineering or Mathematics (BSc, MSc, PhD)	2008–2016	NUTS 2	I
Erasmus	Number of students participating in mobility programmes	Number of students leave/arrive to study abroad (by mobility programme) in the relevant field	2008–2013	NUTS 2	I
GRID	Distribution of educational institutions	Number of educational institutions	–	NUTS 2	I
Labour market					
Eurostat	Employment in technology and knowledge-intensive sectors	Employment in the technology and knowledge-intensive sectors by NUTS 2 regions and sex (from 2008 onwards, NACE Rev. 2) (htec_emp_reg2)	2008–2018	NUTS 2	I
GDELT	Distribution of I4.0-related media appearances	Number of articles published concerning I4.0 in the media by NUTS 2 regions	2018	NUTS 2	I
GRID	Distribution of institutions by categories	Distribution of companies	–	NUTS 2	I

Table 3.9 Analysed indicators grouped by the field supporting regional development (Innovation activities, Technological readiness and Investment) (I-Included, D-Discarded)

Source	Indicator	Definition	Time horizon	Spatial horizon	Used
Innovation activities					
Eurostat	Human Resources in Science and Technology	HRST by category and NUTS 2 regions (hrst_st_rcat)	2008–2018	NUTS 2	I
Regional Innovation Scoreboard (RIS)	Innovative SMEs collaborating with others as a percentage of SMEs	This indicator measures the degree to which SMEs are involved in innovation co-operation. The indicator measures the flow of knowledge between public research institutions and firms, as well as between firms and other firms	NUTS 1 and 2 for different countries	NUTS 1 and 2 for different countries	D
Eurostat	Employment in the technology and knowledge-intensive sectors	Employment in the technology and knowledge-intensive sectors by NUTS 2 regions and sex (from 2008 onwards, NACE Rev. 2) (htec_emp_reg2)	2008–2018	NUTS 2	I
USPTO	Patents	Number of patent applications in the relevant field by regions	2008–2018	NUTS 2	I
CORDIS	Collaboration intensity	Cooperation in the name of the H2020 project between regions	2014–2018	NUTS 2	D
MA-Graph	Publications by categories	Number of publications (at least two I4.0-related topic included)	2008–2018	NUTS 2	I

Technological readiness					
Eurostat	Employment in the technology and knowledge-intensive sectors	Employment in the technology and knowledge-intensive sectors by NUTS 2 regions and sex (from 2008 onwards, NACE Rev. 2) (htec_emp_reg2)	2008–2018	NUTS 2	I
ETER	Graduates in IT, Engineering or Mathematics (BSc, MSc, PhD)	Number of graduates in IT, Engineering or Mathematics. (BSc, MSc, PhD)	2008–2016	NUTS 2	I
MA-Graph	Publications by categories	Number of publications (at least two I4.0 -related topic included)	2008–2018	NUTS 2	I
USPTO	Patents	Number of patent applications in the relevant field by regions	2008–2018	NUTS 2	I
Investment					
Eurostat	Total intramural R&D expenditure	Intramural R&D expenditure (GERD) by sectors of performance and NUTS 2 regions (rd_e_gerdreg)	2008–2016	NUTS 2	I
Eurostat	Total R&D personnel and researchers	Total R&D personnel and researchers by sectors of performance, sex and NUTS 2 regions (rd_p_persreg)	2008–2016	NUTS 2	I

3.4 Discussion

Our main objective was to create an indicator system which can measure I4.0 readiness at regional level. As a result, an available (open), measurable, NUTS 2 classified and more importantly I4.0 specific dataset was created.

References

1. Cordis. https://cordis.europa.eu/datalab/datalab.php?cfg=organizations&menu=collaboration#. Last accessed: 30 November 2019.
2. Cultural and creative cities (c3). https://ec.europa.eu/jrc/en/publication/eur-scientific-and-technical-research-reports/cultural-and-creative-cities-monitor-2019-edition. Last accessed: 30 November 2019.
3. Erasmus+ program. https://acro.ceu.edu/erasmus-mobility-program. Last accessed: 30 November 2019.
4. Eter (european tertiary education register). https://eter-project.com/#/home. Last accessed: 30 November 2019.
5. Eurostat database. https://ec.europa.eu/eurostat/data/database. Last accessed: 30 November 2019.
6. Eurostat Dataset – employment in technology and knowledge-intensive sectors by NUTS 2 regions and sex (from 2008 onwards, nace rev. 2) (htec_emp_reg2). https://ec.europa.eu/eurostat/estat-navtree-portlet-prod/BulkDownloadListing?file=data/htec_emp_reg2.tsv.gz. Last accessed: 30 November 2019.
7. Eurostat Dataset – employment rates of young people not in education and training by sex, educational attainment level, years since completion of highest level of education and NUTS 2 regions (edat_lfse_33). https://ec.europa.eu/eurostat/estat-navtree-portlet-prod/BulkDownloadListing?file=data/edat_lfse_33.tsv.gz. Last accessed: 30 November 2019.
8. Eurostat Dataset – HRST by category and NUTS 2 regions (hrst_st_rcat). https://ec.europa.eu/eurostat/estat-navtree-portlet-prod/BulkDownloadListing?file=data/hrst_st_rcat.tsv.gz. Last accessed: 30 November 2019.
9. Eurostat Dataset – intramural R&D expenditure (GERD) by sectors of performance and NUTS 2 regions (rd_e_gerdreg). https://ec.europa.eu/eurostat/estat-navtree-portlet-prod/BulkDownloadListing?file=data/rd_e_gerdreg.tsv.gz. Last accessed: 30 November 2019.
10. Eurostat Dataset – population aged 25-64 by educational attainment level, sex and NUTS 2 regions (%) (edat_lfse_04). https://ec.europa.eu/eurostat/estat-navtree-portlet-prod/BulkDownloadListing?file=data/edat_lfse_04.tsv.gz. Last accessed: 30 November 2019.
11. Eurostat Dataset – population aged 30–34 by educational attainment level, sex and NUTS 2 regions (%) (edat_lfse_12). https://ec.europa.eu/eurostat/estat-navtree-portlet-prod/BulkDownloadListing?file=data/edat_lfse_12.tsv.gz. Last accessed: 30 November 2019.
12. Eurostat Dataset – population on 1 January by age, sex and NUTS 2 region (demo_r_d2jan). https://ec.europa.eu/eurostat/estat-navtree-portlet-prod/BulkDownloadListing?file=data/demo_r_d2jan.tsv.gz. Last accessed: 30 November 2019.
13. Eurostat Dataset – total R&D personnel and researchers by sectors of performance, sex and NUTS 2 regions (rd_p_persreg). https://ec.europa.eu/eurostat/estat-navtree-portlet-prod/BulkDownloadListing?file=data/rd_p_persreg.tsv.gz. Last accessed: 30 November 2019.
14. Global research identifier database (GRID). https://www.grid.ac/. Last accessed: 30 November 2019.

15. Manda, M. I., & Ben Dhaou, S. (2019, April). Responding to the challenges and opportunities in the 4th industrial revolution in developing countries. In *Proceedings of the 12th International Conference on Theory and Practice of Electronic Governance* (pp. 244–253). New York: ACM.
16. Microsoft academic graph (MA graph). https://www.microsoft.com/en-us/research/project/microsoft-academic-graph/. Last accessed: 30 November 2019.
17. Regional competitiveness index (RCI). https://ec.europa.eu/regional_policy/en/information/publications/working-papers/2019/the-european-regional-competitiveness-index-2019. Last accessed: 30 November 2019.
18. Regional innovation scoreboard (RIS). https://ec.europa.eu/growth/industry/innovation/facts-figures/regional_en. Last accessed: 30 November 2019.
19. The GDELT project. https://www.gdeltproject.org/. Last accessed: 30 November 2019.
20. United states patent and trademark office (USPTO). https://patents.reedtech.com/patent-products.php. Last accessed: 30 November 2019.

Chapter 4
Evaluation of Regional I4.0 Readiness: Data Analysis and Composite Indicator Development

4.1 Characteristics of Regional Indicator Systems

Before going into details of the analysis of the previously presented data, we pay attention to other regional indicator systems and their field of applicability. Even though in Sect. 3.1.2, some of the relevant indicators were interpreted, now their core dimensions and the structure of indicators will also be highlighted.

Tables 4.1 and 4.2 show the regional indicator systems, their observed topics and application possibilities.

1. Regional Competitiveness Index 2019 (RCI):[1] It observes 28 EU Member States including 268 regions at the NUTS 2 level. There are 11 dimensions of competitiveness, including 74 indicators which are connected to productivity and long-term development. Most of the indicators are available with in the 2015–2017 time horizon [2].

   RCI uses Principal Component Analysis (PCA) "in composite index construction when each pillar in a composite index is meant to describe a particular aspect of the latent phenomenon to be measured, in this case, regional competitiveness". These phenomena cannot be measured directly, and are only observable with the use of indicators and proxies which can describe them.
2. Regional Innovation Scoreboard 2019 (RIS):[2] The spatial horizon observed at the NUTS 2 level in 23 EU Member States, Norway, Serbia and Switzerland, including 238 regions. Furthermore on a national level, Cyprus, Estonia, Latvia, Luxembourg and Malta are identical to NUTS 1 or NUTS 2 level according to their territories.

   Seventeen indicators also used in EIS 2019 are applied. These are grouped into four types, namely Framework conditions, Investment, Innovation activities

[1] https://ec.europa.eu/regional_policy/sources/docgener/work/2019_03_rci2019.pdf.

[2] https://ec.europa.eu/growth/industry/innovation/facts-figures/regional_en.

J. Abonyi et al., *Are Regions Prepared for Industry 4.0?*, SpringerBriefs in Entrepreneurship and Innovation, https://doi.org/10.1007/978-3-030-53103-4_4

Table 4.1 The characteristics and applicability of regional indicator systems I

Indicator system	No.	Theme		GEO level	Definition	Application
RCI '19	1.	Institutions	Regional	NUTS 2/1/0	European Commission's Regional Competitiveness Index (RCI) is to be published some 10 years after the global financial crisis, with the world economy showing signs of recovery	The RCI should be considered as an instrument to assist with the design of better policies and monitoring their effectiveness.
			National	Country		
	2.	Macroeconomic stability		Country		
	3.	Infrastructure		NUTS 2		
	4.	Health		NUTS 2		
	5.	Basic education country		Country		
	6.	Higher education and LLL		NUTS 2		
	7.	Labour market efficiency		NUTS 2		
	8.	Market size		NUTS 2		
	9.	Technological readiness	Regional	NUTS 2		
			National	Country		
	10.	Business sophistication		NUTS 2		
	11.	Innovation		NUTS 2		

RIS '19	1.	Population with a tertiary education		NUTS 2	The European Innovation Scoreboard (EIS) provides a comparative analysis of innovation performance in EU countries, other European countries, and regional neighbours. It assesses relative strengths and weaknesses of national innovation systems and helps countries identify areas they need to address	It provides a more detailed breakdown of performance groups with contextual data that can be used to analyse and compare structural economic, business and socio-demographic structural differences between regions
	2.	Lifelong Learning		NUTS 2		
	3.	Scientific co-publications		NUTS 2		
	4.	Most-cited publications		NUTS 2		
	5.	R&D expenditure public sector		NUTS 2		
	6.	R&D expenditure business sector		NUTS 2		
	7.	Non-R&D innovation expenditures		NUTS 2 /1		
	8.	Product or process innovators		NUTS 2 /1		
	9.	Marketing or organisational innovators		NUTS 2 /1		
	10.	SMEs innovation in-house		NUTS 2 /1		
	11.	Innovative SMEs collaborating with others		NUTS 2 /1		
	12.	Public-private co-publications		NUTS 2		
	13.	PCT patent applications		NUTS 2		
	14.	Trademark applications		NUTS 2		
	15.	Design applications		NUTS 2		
	16.	Employment in MHT manufacturing and knowledge-intensive services		NUTS 2		
	17.	Sales of new-to-market and new-to-firm innovations		NUTS 2 /1		

(continued)

Table 4.1 (continued)

Indicator system	No.	Theme		GEO level	Definition	Application
C3	1.	Cultural vibrancy			A tool designed to monitor and benchmark the performance of cultural and creative cities in Europe	Allows cities and local stakeholders to monitor progress over time
		Cultural venues and facilities		City		
		Cultural participation and attractiveness		City		
	2.	Creative economy				
		Creative and knowledge-based jobs		City		
		Intellectual property and innovation		NUTS 2/ 3		
		New jobs in creative sectors		NUTS 3		
	3.	Enabling environment				
		Human capital and education		City		
		Openness, tolerance and trust		City		
		Quality of governance		NUTS 2/ 1/ 0		

Table 4.2 The characteristics and applicability of regional indicator systems II

Indicator system	No.	Theme	GEO level	Definition	Application
SDEWES Index	D1	Energy usage and climate	City	The sustainable development of energy, water, and environment systems (SDEWES) index benchmarks cities based on 7 dimensions, 35 main indicators, and about 25 sub-indicators	Benchmarking the performance of cities across metrics related to energy, water and environment systems presents an opportunity to trigger policy learning, action, and cooperation to bring cities closer to sustainable development
	D2	Penetration of energy and CO2-saving measures	City		
	D3	Renewable energy potential and utilization	City		
	D4	Water usage and environmental quality	City		
	D5	CO2 emissions and industrial profile	City		
	D6	Urban planning and social welfare	City		
	D7	R&D, innovation and sustainability policy	City		

(continued)

Table 4.2 (continued)

Indicator system	No.	Theme	GEO level	Definition	Application
OECD—Regional well-being	1.	Safety	NUTS 2	This interactive site allows you to measure well-being in your region and compare it with 402 other OECD regions based on eleven topics central to the quality of our lives	Comparable measures of regional well-being offer a new way to gauge what policies work and can empower a community to act to achieve higher well-being for its citizens
	2.	Housing	NUTS 2		
	3.	Life satisfaction	NUTS 2		
	4.	Access to services	NUTS 2		
	5.	Civic engagement	NUTS 2		
	6.	Education	NUTS 2		
	7.	Jobs	NUTS 2		
	8.	Community	NUTS 2		
	9.	Environment	NUTS 2		
	10.	Income	NUTS 2		
	11.	Health	NUTS 2		
KRAFT	1.	Creativity and potential in innovation, ability to create knowledge,	Cities and regions	It is a complex system which measures the potential in networks and connections, the social as well as relational capital, and the sustainable potential by not only using "hard" indicators, but bringing "soft" factors to the fore	It is aimed to support decision-making and foster knowledge intensity both in private sector, for territorial councils whose want to step into the "global world-map", knowledge centric universities and research centers and also for national and European level governance
	2.	Social and relational capital, network potential and "interconnectivity"			
	3.	Potential in sustainability			

and Impact, including ten dimensions overall. RIS measures average innovation performance by the use of a composite indicator called Regional Innovation Index (RII). It is calculated as the unweighted average of the normalised scores of the 17 indicators.

Regions are classified into four innovation performance groups, namely Leaders, Strong Innovators, Moderate Innovators and Modest Innovators. (Each group is split into + and − according to their trends [5].)

3. Cultural and Creative Cities Monitor 2019 (C3):[3] C3 refers to 190 cities in 30 European countries (28 that belong to the EU along with Norway and Switzerland).

   This tool is based on both qualitative and quantitative methods. According to the latter, 29 indicators were chosen and categorized into nine dimensions. These dimensions can be classified into three major groups: the city's cultural vibrancy, creative economy, and enabling environment. The C3 Index is calculated as a weighted average of the aforementioned sub-index scores of the three significant groups (CV 40%, CE 40%, EE 20%). The qualitative method is based on the creative economy strategies of cities. This composite indicator aim to monitor and assess the performance of 'Cultural and Creative Cities' [4].

4. Sustainable Development of Energy, Water and Environment Systems (SDEWES):[4] the SDEWES Index has been applied to 120 cities "which correspond to samples of South-East European cities, Mediterranean port cities, and other cities around the world based on multiple criteria to increase geographical diversity".

   The Index is based on seven dimensions, which can be broken down into 35 main-, and 25 sub-indicators. Each dimension includes five main indicators which have been normalized, and these create an aggregated index value. The SDEWES City Index Atlas is a spatial visualization of the ranked system. Cities have been categorized into Challenged, Solution-seeking, Transitioning and Pioneer Cities.

5. OECD—Regional Well-Being:[5] This tool compares closely 400 OECD regions according to the set of indicators. There are 11 topics which are aimed to determine both the material conditions as well as quality of life. Each topic includes one or two indicators, normalised using the Min-Max method which ranges from 0 to 10. (If more than one indicator falls within the topic, the scores are aggregated.)

6. KRAFT Index: Creative Cities—Sustainable Regions [6] is a complex system which measures the potential in networks and connections, social and relational capital, as well as sustainable potential by not only using "hard" indicators but bringing "soft" factors to the fore. In order to determine the economic development and competitiveness of a region, it evaluates the quality of life,

[3] https://ec.europa.eu/jrc/en/publication/eur-scientific-and-technical-research-reports/cultural-and-creative-cities-monitor-2019-edition.

[4] https://www.sdewes.org/sdewes_index.php.

[5] https://www.oecdregionalwellbeing.org/.

labour demand and sustainable factors in a region. “KRAFT formula”: $X = C^x L^{\alpha x} K^{\beta x} R^{\gamma}$, where x denotes the output of the city and region, L stands for the labour force, *K* represents the capital, *R* denotes relevant factors as knowledge, and α, β, γ are parameters.

4.2 Construction of Composite Indicators

4.2.1 Methodological Steps of Composite Indicator Development

“Composite indicators are aggregations of observable variables, which aim to quantify concepts that are not directly observable, such as competitiveness, freedom of press or climate hazards.” The usage of composite indicators and some methodological steps were mentioned in Sect. 4.1, although as clarification the overall method for constructing composite indicator is discussed in this section. Joint Research Centre (JRC)[6] is the Commission’s in-house science service. By providing developed methodologies for building composite indicators, the work of policy-makers is eased by helping to monitor progress and shape policy in areas like lifelong learning or competitiveness.

JRC has been working on composite indicators since 2002. It cooperates with policy departments known as Directorates-General, to deal with social challenges by developing methods, standards and tools. Furthermore, JRC, along with OECD, has developed a handbook (“Handbook on Constructing Composite Indicators: Methodology and User Guide”) for practitioners concerning how to build a composite indicator.

They have developed a commonly used methodology/“checklist” for constructing composite indicators. This concept, namely the main steps and examples or commonly used methods, is shown in Fig. 4.1.

Indicator systems have been created to identify the current (reference year/temporal horizon) economic, social or environmental conditions. In the spatial horizon, it can be applied to cities, territories, regions (NUTS), countries, continents or even worldwide. The main aim is to understand a given complex topic by its categorised indicators. It As a result, the gaps and connections between variables are measured and suggestions made for usage.

Composite indicators integrate information from several areas, which reflects the economy, society or environment as well as their correlations and effects. It measure a multidimensional concept that single indicators are unable to determine.

Although we have to bear in mind how methods effect our composite indicator, and how it changes according to the field of usage. Even at the beginning, the theoretical framework and selection or combination of variables need to be suitable

[6] https://composite-indicators.jrc.ec.europa.eu/?q=about-us.

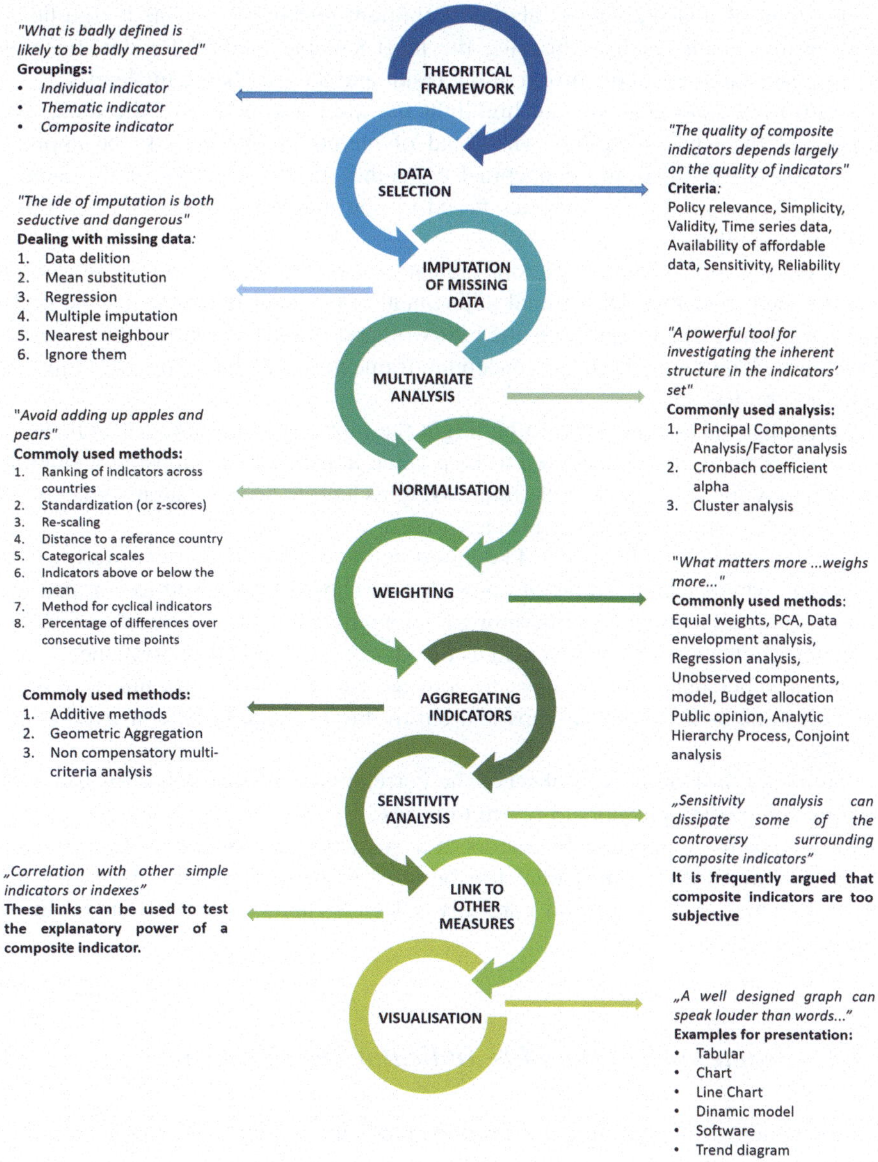

Fig. 4.1 Guidance for constructing composite indicators

for the purpose. It may apply that the more comprehensive the indicator, weakly it reflects the actual area. The field of study must be approached specifically.

On the other hand, we must take into consideration the availability of the selected variables according to what do we want to measure at which spatial and temporal horizon. Criteria must match the purpose of the measurement.

The issue of missing data is also an important question as it has a significant effect on the given results. Choosing the most suitable method for dealing with missing data can prevent distortion of the result and the user being mislead.

Multivariate data analysis can highlight the hidden structure of the data. The purpose of the study identifies what kind of methodology needs to be applied, e.g. to assess statistical and conceptual coherence in the structure of the dataset or identify peer groups of countries based on the individual indicators and other auxiliary variables.

For the purpose of normalization, indicators were applied on a common scale to make them rankable. Directional adjustment is essential to determine the highest/lowest value, which represents the best/worst performance. During the selection of the normalization method, the conceptual framework and data properties must be easily interpreted.

Weighting makes it possible to highlight the effect or importance of indicators; on the other hand, it is considered to be a value judgement so choosing a suitable methodology for the purpose is essential. Weights have to be transparent and explicit for the users to ensure the system is easy to use.

The aggregation method should be based on the concept to be measured, which "considers whether high values of one indicator should be allowed to compensate for low values of another". Furthermore, after aggregation, the relationship with the underlying indicators can be revealed as this drives good or bad performance.

On the other hand, we do have to consider the sensitivity and uncertainty of the indicators, as it can reveal gaps and ensure the message to be conveyed is not damaged.

One of the last steps is to observe the correlations between other measures or existing composite indicators to reveal linkages.

Presenting the composite indicators is a great way to communicate the given results and make them transparent for the user. Visualization has to be fit for the target audience and useful and carefully selected charts as well as information interpreted clearly.

4.2.2 Framework of the I40+ Indicator Development

The methodology of analysing the developed indicator system and to rank variables is shown in Fig. 4.2.

The I4.0+ indicator system is analysed with both SRD (Sum of Ranking Differences) and Promethee method. SRD [3] describes a probability distribution function and indicates the distances of each variables from the ideal, reference condition which are ranked according to the reference (the most relevant first). It is an excellent method for identifying which indicators are the most forward to describe our concept and which are more backward and ranked in reverse. The details of the SRD method are described in Appendix A.

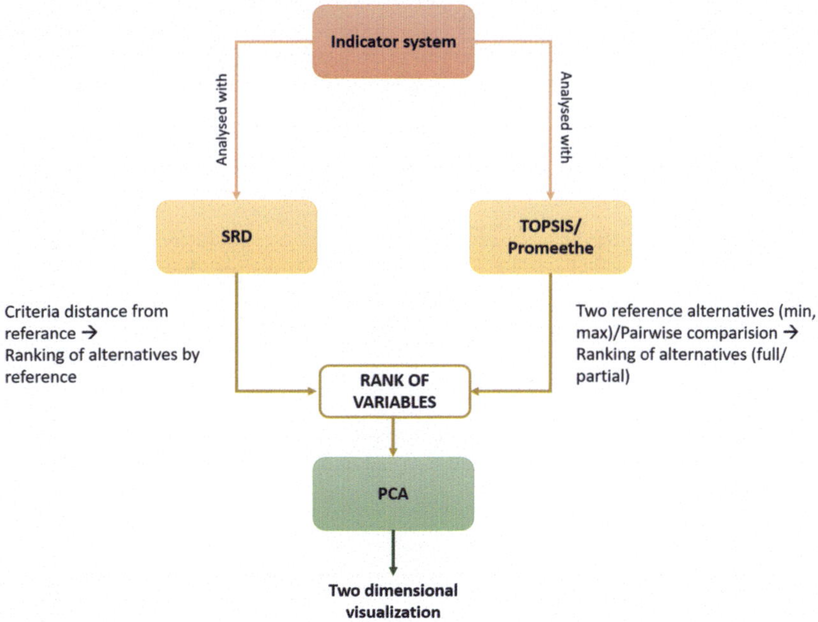

Fig. 4.2 Analysing methodologies used for ranking variables and determining correlations

Promethee II [1] makes a pairwise comparison according to the criteria. It creates the full or partial ranking of alternatives. Visualisation takes place in accordance with the Promethee-Gaia method and principal component analysis of decision-making processes (preferences) calculated by criteria. The Promethee II method is described in Appendix B.

Following analysis of the indicators, regions were indicated in a two-dimensional space, based on Principal Component Analysis (PCA). The two main components determine the locations of the regions; therefore, it can be qualified as a composite indicator.

4.3 Application Study: Readiness in the European Union

In this section, the aforementioned methodologies are applied for the developed I4.0+ indicator system. Firstly, the examined indicators are analysed with SRD method, which are shown in Fig. 4.3. It should be noted that from the selected indicators, we used the latest available data, which can be varied in the time horizon. It is our aspiration to be up-to-date, so the preferred year of availability is 2018, on the other hand, some indicators from open data portals have not been updated since 2016 (GERD, R&D personnel, Number of graduates). The most out-of-date index

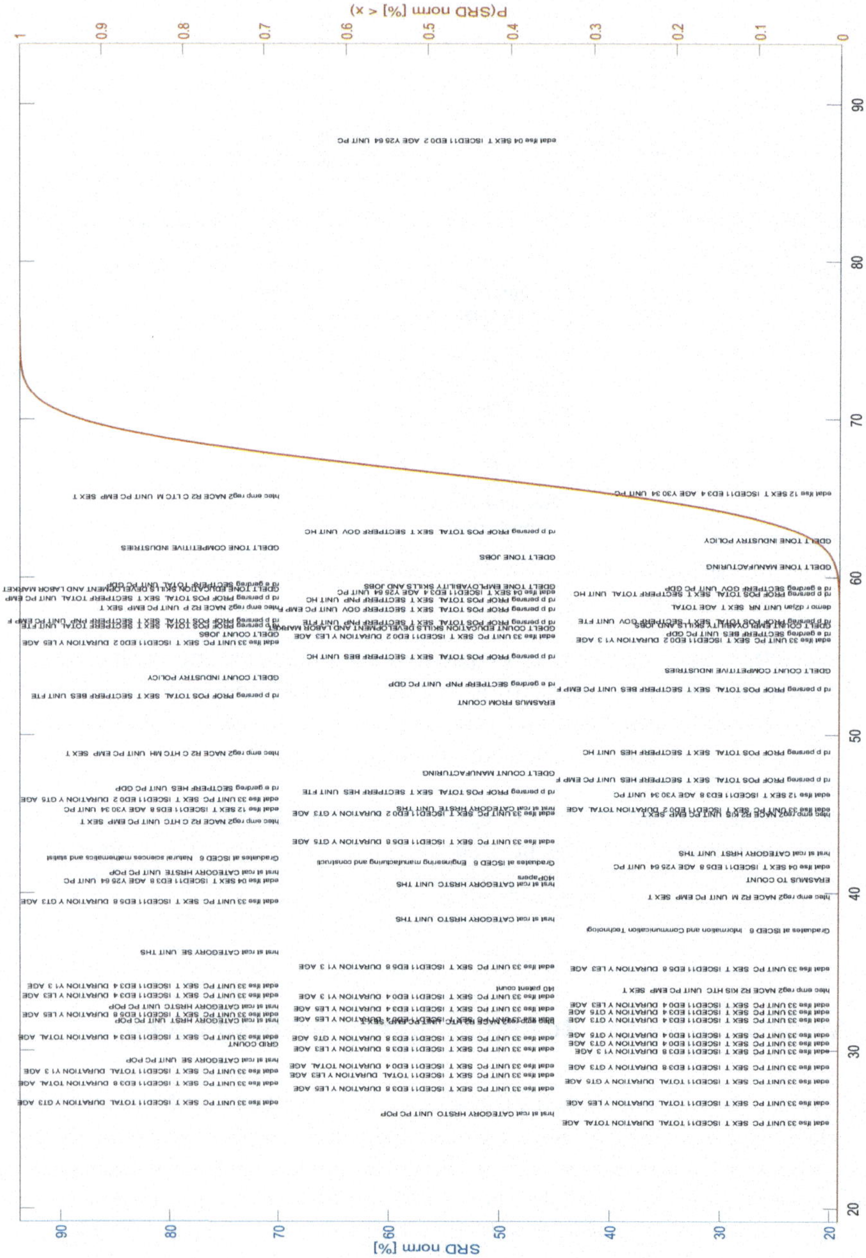

Fig. 4.3 Variables ranked according to the SRD method

is the Erasmus count, as the latest updated data was in 2013. The description of variables are defined in Appendix C.

Concerning the given result, we selected the main components describing I4.0 readiness. These can be seen in Fig. 4.4 by name and ranked on the scale.

It is worth noticing that the zone, which is the closest to the "excellence" measurement, can be categorized into two significant groups. One of them is the employment and its indicators; the other is research and innovation area. The method also highlights the outstanding values which exhibit less of an impact on regional readiness.

The employment-related variables indicate the importance of and connection with education and innovation, as there is an increasing need for a qualified workforce and scientific activities.

1. Total Employment rates of young people not in education and training includes all educational levels and education from the age of 15–34. They measures the number of people employed after finishing education.

   Even though it can be qualified by itself, on the other hand, with our concept, it can represent an added value. It is important to determine whether this variable is a cause or effect. It can reflect a developed economy as job opportunities exist and economic value is generated in a region.

   It is clearly visible that its sub-indicators are also listed between approximately the 25–35 horizontal line, which underlines the importance of the total employment rates of young people.

The second significant group highlighted is the research and innovation area, which also correlates with the labour, education and technology factor. This is underlined by the presence of the people employed in science and technology indicator as well as employment in the high-technology sector. Furthermore, investment also plays a significant role in the research and innovation area.

2. Human Resources in Science and Technology under the category of Persons employed in science and technology is the following indicator which most closely measures excellence in the field.

   It measures the percentage of the total population employed in science and technology and reflects that there is an emerging need for researchers and scientific actions.
3. The density of research institutions is one of the following relevant variables, as it measures the number of institutions involved in research activities.
4. Human Resources in Science and Technology under the category of Scientists and engineers. As has been mentioned before, the employment rate in science and technology plays an important role in development. This indicator is one of its sub-indicators, so its relevance is highlighted even more.
5. Employment in the High-technology sectors (high-technology manufacturing and knowledge-intensive high-technology services) measures those people employed as a percentage of total employment. It indicates the demand of

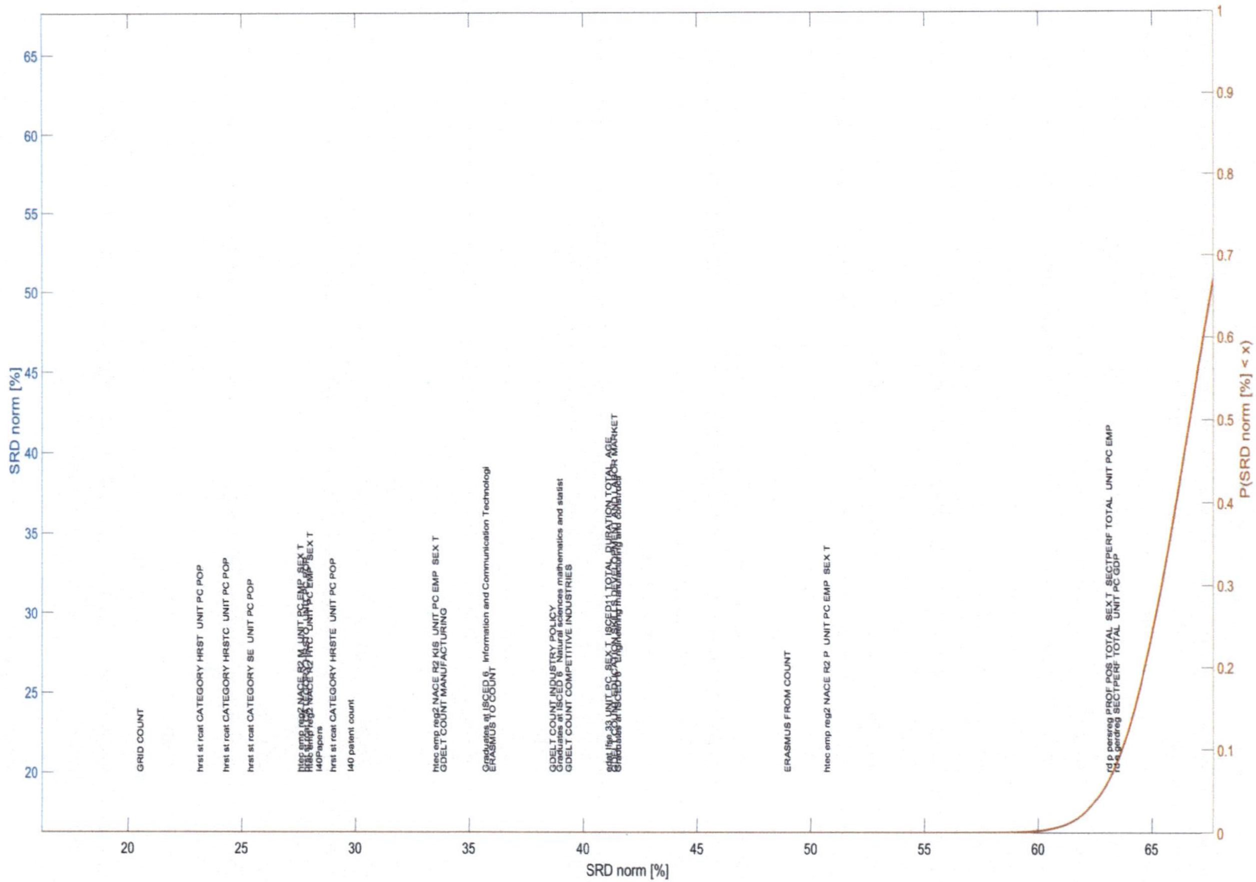

Fig. 4.4 Selected variables from the SRD method according to their relevance in terms of measurements

the labour market in the field, which reflects how regions keep up with advanced technologies.

6. Industry 4.0-related publications are also heading in the direction of research activities and indicate regional maturity in terms of how much a given region is working on I4.0 (research) projects.
7. Industry 4.0-related patent applications approximate the trend of the human resources in science and technology indicator. It is unequivocal that they are strongly correlated as the number people working in science and technology is the reason for the density of patent applications (effect) within a region. It can identify the research activity and innovation capability of a region.
8. The appearance of Industry 4.0-related news is located over one third of the scale as is the case quite close to the reference. It is fascinating that the Intramural R&D expenditures (GERD) are located on the same scale, next to the appearance of news. Consequently, we can claim that the use of GDELT can function as a "proxy" indicator and make an assumption of how much is spent by sectors on research and development actions. It should even be noted that according to the Eurostat database, the latest available data on GERD dates back to 2016, while the available news on GDELT is updated continuously.

   On the other hand, while the count of news has a significant effect, its tone does not have an added value for the index.

As has been mentioned, the outliers highlight those factors which are less relevant in terms of measuring regional readiness. As it is shown in Fig. 4.3, one of the outstanding indexes is the Population aged 25–64 in the educational level of less than primary, primary and lower secondary (%). According to its location in the generated coordinate system, it can approximated to a random variable.

Figure 4.5 shows the ranking according to the Promethee II method. It is clear that the indicators that point the furthest in the same way are the most determinative. Appendix C indicate the description of the indicators.

This also underlines the statement according to the SRD method that the two main leading groups of indicators can be categorised as (1) employment and (2) research and innovation actions. In this case, these factors are the Human Resources in Science and Technology, Total Employment rates of young people not in education and training, Employment in technology and knowledge-intensive sectors, and the Total R&D personnel and researchers.

The horizontal axis of the PCA refers to regional development, while the vertical axis is connected to the innovative feature of the given region. A visual interpretation can be seen in Fig. 4.6. The more developed regions are located on a Pareto chart.

This ranking has been applied to world map as seen in Fig. 4.7. According to the ranking, the most developed region is located in southern Finland, in the Helsinki-Uusimaa region, followed by the region of the capital city of the Czech Republic, Prague and of Germany, Berlin.

In Fig. 4.7, the ranking of regional I4.0 readiness in European regions can be seen based on the Promethee method.

Fig. 4.5 Selected factors according to their importance in the Promethee-Gaia method

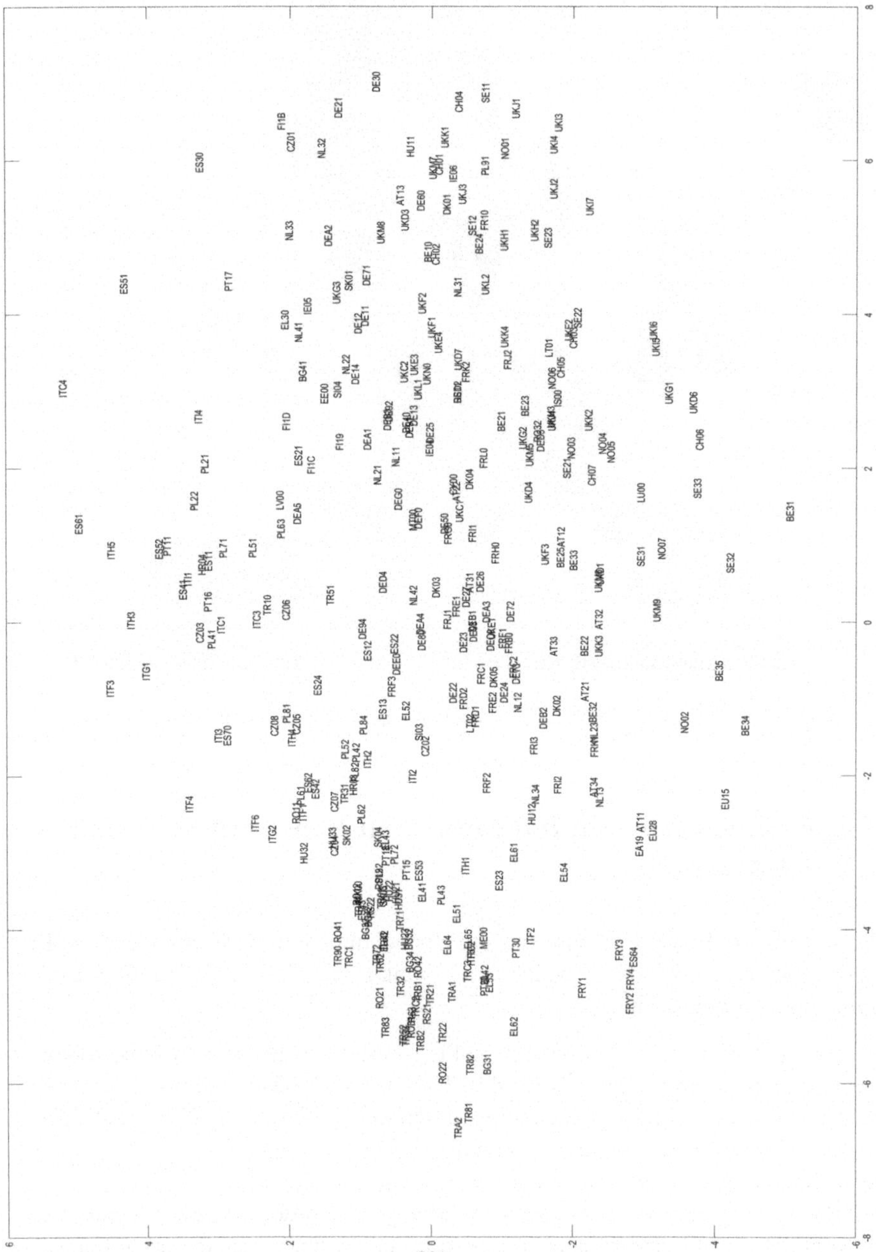

Fig. 4.6 The layout of regions according to the PCA method as an indication of regional readiness

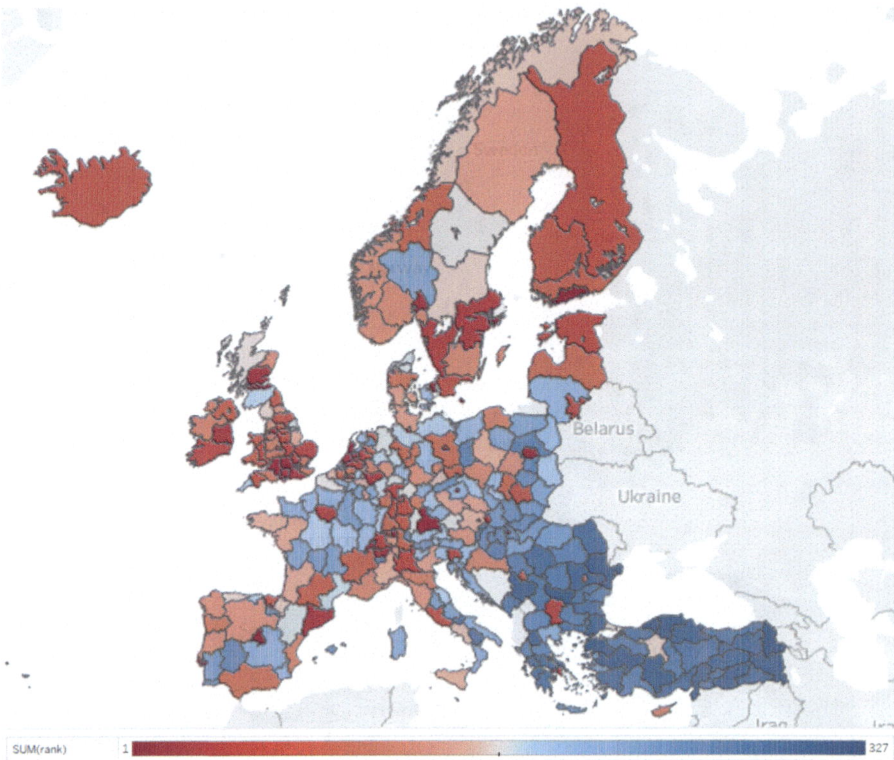

Fig. 4.7 The ranking of European NUTS 2 regional I4.0 readiness based on the Promethee method

4.4 Correlation Between Indicators that Represent Economic Development

In this section firstly we compare the developed indicator with other economic indicators, then existing indexes which aim to rank regions according to innovation capability and competitiveness.

1. Comparing our regional innovation ranking system to the GDP of the region is essential to identify the relationship between European regional economic growth and the regional I4.0 ranking based on the Promethee method. The results yield a 0.68 correlation between them, which is indicative of a connection between economic development and our proposed methodology.

   Industry 4.0 started as a German strategy in order to boost economic development; on the other hand, it has to be noted that other factors influence GDP as well. In this regard, it is hard to identify the developing effect of I4.0 on economic growth.

Figure 4.8 underlines the fact that there are regions which have a relatively high GDP compared to our index, as their economic growth originates from other factors unrelated to I4.0.

2. The relationship between regional development (Real growth rate of regional gross value added (GVA)) and the proposed innovation index reflects that regions which are more backward, according to our ranking, are capable of improving without the application of the I4.0 concept by investing in the future. While regions which do not take further steps to develop regionally and improve their overall economic prosperity are unable to emerge.
3. According to the Regional Innovation Scoreboard 2019 (RIS) report, and its composite indicator, the Regional Innovation Index (RII), which is used to measure the average innovation performance, we also correlated it with ours.

   Figure 4.9 shows the linkage between the two indexes, the correlation of which is 0.70. It is a fair representation of the similarity that points in the same

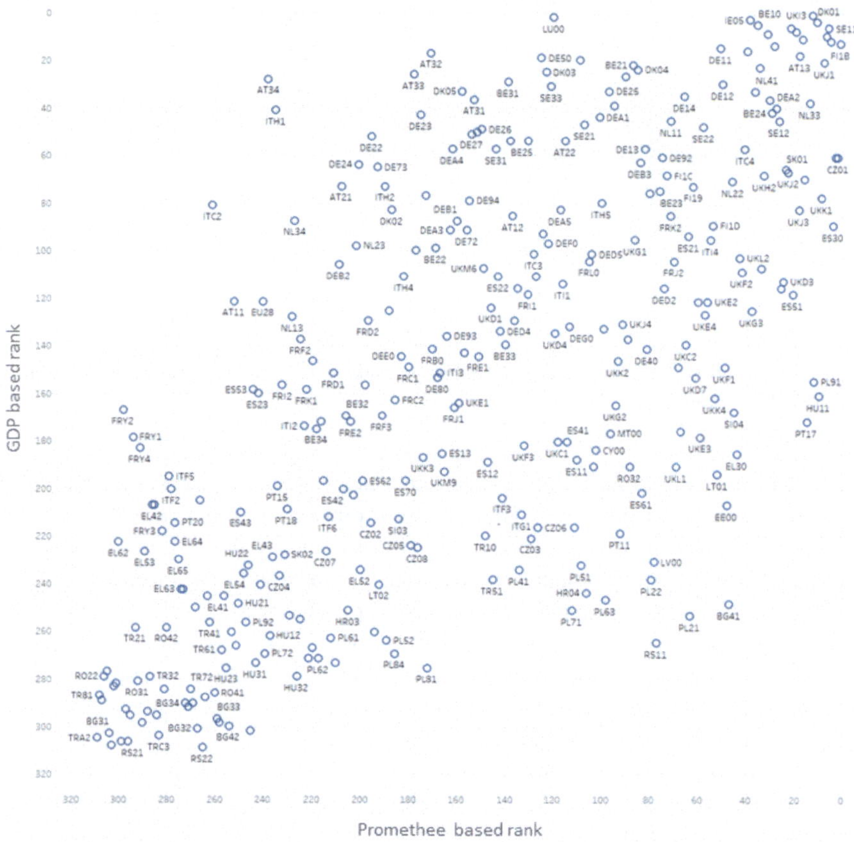

Fig. 4.8 The correlation between GDP and our I4.0+ ranking system ($r^2 = 0.68$)

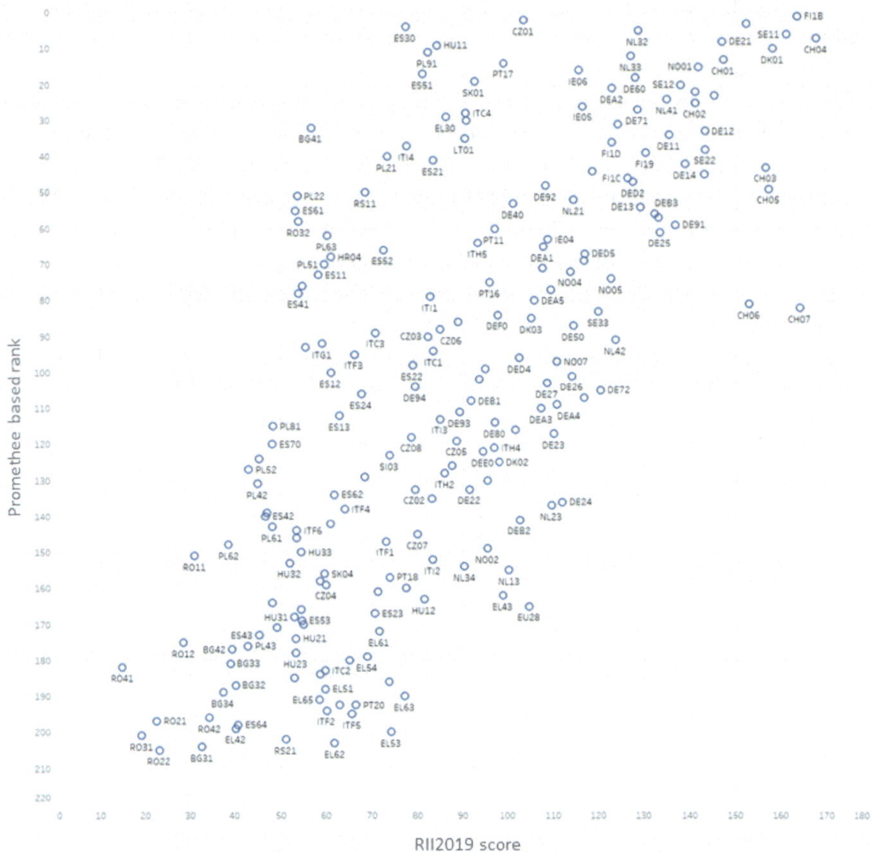

Fig. 4.9 The correlation between the proposed I4.0+ ranking index and the Regional Innovation Index (RII) ($r^2 = 0.70$)

direction. The horizontal and vertical axes are reflect on innovation and I4.0 specific features, respectively. This clearly represents regions considered to be moderate innovators, in order to advance to the next level, the governmental focus is strongly on the development of innovation and improving the application of the I4.0 concept. These regions are located above the diagonal.

4. We can not pass by the comparison with the Regional Competitiveness Index, as competitiveness provides a basis for a stable soil in which to apply the I4.0 concept. By comparing the two indexes, a correlation of 0.70 was calculated. Figure 4.10 represents this relation.

   It is worth noticing that there are regions where the implementation of I4.0 is not a priority, even though they still belong to the competitive regions such as regions of AT and LU.

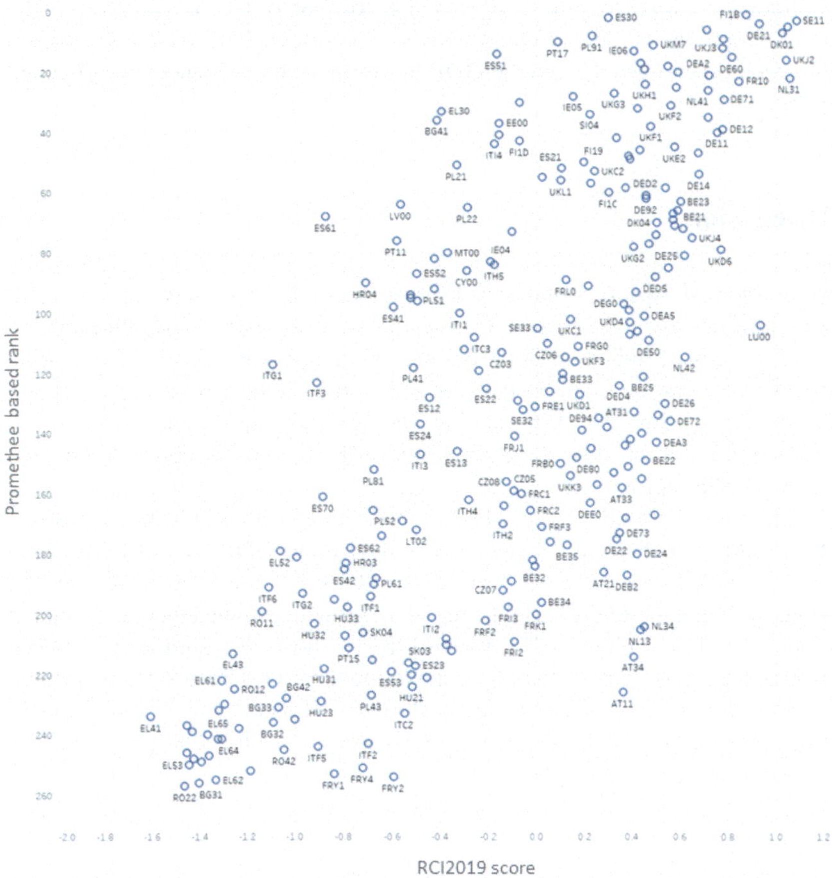

Fig. 4.10 The correlation between the proposed I4.0+ ranking index and the Regional Competitiveness Index (RCI) ($r^2 = 0.70$)

In conclusion, it can be claimed that the proposed readiness index reflects both regional development and the innovation capability (can be as one of its factors). Indicators were categorised according to five main dimensions (higher education and lifelong learning, labour market, innovation activities, investment and technological readiness), positive relationships of which between each other and the fostering effect can be stated according to the results. It is clearly visible that regions are arranged according to two main areas, namely employment and innovation factors.

By comparing the proposed index with already existing indicator systems, which measure competitiveness and innovation, the correlation between them was almost 0.7, which is indicative of their similarity and connections.

Furthermore, the linkage with GDP was also correlated (0.68), which raises the question of which one is the cause and which is the effect. Both have a significant impact on each other, even though the GDP has more of an influence, even beyond I4.0 capabilities.

4.5 Discussion

To measure regional aspects of industry 4.0 readiness a NUTS 2 level I4.0 regional ranking system has been developed. During the analysis (both SRD, Promethee), two leading groups of indicators were defined: (1) employment and (2) education and innovation. It can be claimed that the innovation-helix actors role is critical and necessary. Regarding the I4.0+ ranking, the most advanced region is Helsinki-Uusimaa, which is followed by the capital city of the Czech Republic, Prague and the German, Berlin region.

The comparison with GDP showed 0.68 correlation, which indicates a positive correlation (although there are many factors determine GDP as well). Regional development related connection reflects that I4.0 is not the only factor needed to improve, although without a stable regional growth cannot emerge. Regional innovation index is correlated 0.70, which clearly shows the similarity between the two indexes. It is visible that by innovation and I4.0 focused government focus, regions are stepping ahead to break through. The correlation with regional competitiveness index is 0.70. The similarity is unequivocal as competitiveness is the nutritious soil of I4.0 concept.

References

1. Brans, J. P., & Mareschal, B. (1992). Promethee v: Mcdm problems with segmentation constraints. *INFOR: Information Systems and Operational Research, 30*(2), 85–96.
2. Dijkstra, L., & Annoni, P. (2019). *Regional competitiveness index 2019* (pp. 1–29). European Commission.
3. Héberger, K. (2010). Sum of ranking differences compares methods or models fairly. *TrAC Trends in Analytical Chemistry, 29*(1), 101–109.
4. Joint Research Centre. (2019). *The cultural and creative cities monitor* (pp. 1–113). European Commission.
5. Merkelbach, I., Hollanders, H., & Es-Sadki, N. (2019). *European innovation scoreboard 2019* (pp. 1–94). Europan Commission.
6. Miszlivetz, F., & Márkus, E. (2013). A kraft-index–kreatív városok–fenntartható vidék (the kraft index: Creative cities–sustainable regions). *Vezetéstudomány-Budapest Management Review, 44*(9), 2–21.

Chapter 5
Summary: The Applicability of the I4.0+ Index

The major objective of this book was to identify the readiness of region to adapt to the concept of Industry 4.0. The "glocal" aspect was considered during this research as it is believed that this conscious aspiration for industrialization cannot root deeply without regional development, which supports the overall intention of a better quality of life. In this regard an indicator system that refers to the readiness of a region was sought, which can be broadly used by stakeholders.

After the theoretical introduction of the I4.0 concept and its key elements for implementation, the gaps in readiness measurements were also highlighted as the regional aspect had yet to be examined. Even though SMEs and countries have considerable reputations, we can not dismiss the regional perspective and its development.

Our proposed indicator system was categorised into five dimensions, namely higher education and lifelong learning, the labour market, innovation activities, investment and technological readiness. All these segments are strongly correlated with each other and the relevance of the triple helix underlies this even more.

During our research, we were seeking to be up-to-date and using available data sources that are suitable for monitoring regions. This is why both statistical sources and open data portals were used to find the most suitable information for our purpose. From the perspective of spatial coverage, the desired GEO level is the NUTS 2 regional level, which was accomplished, moreover, some of the indicators are able to measure on the city level which provides even more details. Bearing in mind the purpose of measuring I4.0 readiness, the selection of indicators was strongly determined by their specific relation to the area, e.g. I4.0-related publications, patents or educational training. Moreover, the appearance of I4.0-related news was measured at the regional level as well, which was used as a "proxy" indicator to identify the regional connection to the field of study.

This book was aimed to convey a message as well as draw attention to the five dimensions mentioned and their high degree of importance in regional development

J. Abonyi et al., *Are Regions Prepared for Industry 4.0?*, SpringerBriefs in Entrepreneurship and Innovation, https://doi.org/10.1007/978-3-030-53103-4_5

activities, which is also strongly related to the fostering effect of the I4.0 concept. According to the proposed methodology, this also confirms their importance.

Furthermore, it can be stated that the two main driving forces were employment and innovation activities, as regions were ranked according to these two axes using the Promethee method. The most advanced regions in the field of I4.0 readiness are Helsinki-Uusimaa in Finland, Prague in the Czech Republic, then Berlin and Upper Bavaria in Germany.

According to the correlation analysis with the RCI and RII, a correlation of close to 0.7 was observed with the proposed and existing indexes. It can adumbrate the similarity and the fostering effect on each other. On the other hand, the changes in GDP also correlate with our index, even though the GDP can be influenced by several other factors.

Even though indicators can also be used individually, integrating them into a system gives an added value to the concept and makes it possible for multiple usages. It should be noted that the stakeholders can be connected to the triple helix actors as well as governments, business sectors and academia.

It has an untapped potential which can be utilized by governments to stimulate the regional economy, determine strategies for research and innovation projects and take into account the Smart Specialization Strategies among regions. On the other hand, regional/territorial councils can draw conclusions from the regional ranking, determine future aspirations and identify further steps for areas that have to be improved to enhance regional development. From the viewpoint of investors, it can operate as a "heat map" to identify which regions are worth investing in according to their development potential and economic stability. It is also true for entrepreneurs that they can qualify which region is capable of adapting to necessary changes and keep up with the competitive environment.

The proposed I4.0+ readiness index was created for those parties who have aspirations to grow and adopt innovative features that focus on interconnections and cooperation in order to provide a competitive and stable economic region.

Defining the applicability of the proposed index is a critical step, as the interests of possible stakeholders have to be identified and taken into account.

We classified four possible parties as shown in Fig. 5.1, who could benefit from the use of the I4.0+ index and draw conclusion about the status of regional development.

1. Governments have power over regions, not just financially but with policymaking as well. Considering regional economic development, governments can use this index to measure regional statuses and identify future strategic plans for their improvement. This can include research and development allocations, innovation projects or Smart Specialization Strategies (S3) among regions. If a country wants to make its mark on the "global world map", first it has to start to develop on lower levels and keep up with continually changing global requirements.
2. The role of territorial councils is also appreciated as they are directly involved and able to identify what has to improve. The I4.0+ readiness index confirms the position of regions in the ranking. Regions can determine their future

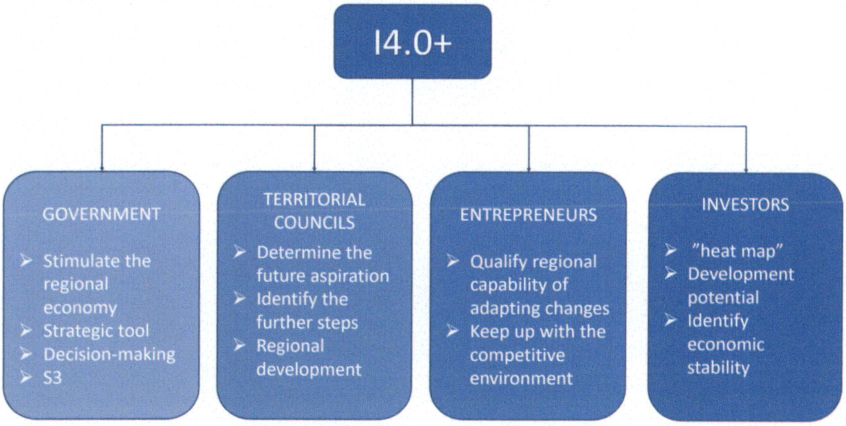

Fig. 5.1 Applicability of the I4.0+ index to utilize the potential of regional strength

aspirations and further steps in order to be competitive regionally and strong economically. The triple helix performance is perform in regional stage, and can create connections between businesses, governments and academia.

3. Entrepreneurs connected to the business sector can use the index as a tool for identifying the capability of regions to remain or become stable. They can see which are worth investing in and how regions are able to develop by the concept of I4.0. The connection of SMEs to this concept is critical as they can function as the potential drivers of economic growth.
4. Investors can use it as a "heat map" to determine which region is worth investing in, or stable enough to cope with future challenges. The area of investment is also critical in terms of research and development, manufacturing or attracting businesses to a region. Each has its own strengths to achieve economic development by either creating new job opportunities, financial funds or relationship between other parties and regions.

Appendix A
The Sum of Ranking Differences (SRD) Method

This chapter presents the steps of the Sum of Ranking Differences (SRD) method used to evaluate how the selected measures provide similar rankings.

SRD is a method of ranking, which is intended to compare models, methods, analytical techniques, panel members, etc. and it is entirely general.

The methodological steps of SRD are presented in Fig. A.1.

- In order to analyse data using the SRD method, data have to be arranged in a matrix form (objects, statistical cases, compounds, etc.) enumerated in the rows, whereas variables (models, methods) to be compared are arranged in the columns.
- In the following, the results are ranked for each model to compare them to the ranking of known or reference values.
- Then the absolute values of the differences between reference and individual rankings are totalled for all models or variables to be compared. The closer the SRD value is to zero (closer to the golden standard) the better is the model is.
- The SRD proximity of values can identify the similarity of the variables (models).
- Generally, in the absence of known or reference results, the average can be accepted as the golden standard (even if bias is also present in the model resulting in an increase in to random errors).
- The SRD method can be validated by using simulated random numbers for comparison (permutation test).
- In the case of a small number of objects ($n < 14$), a recursive algorithm calculates the discrete distribution, while when the number of objects is large ($n > 13$), a normal distribution is used.

J. Abonyi et al., *Are Regions Prepared for Industry 4.0?*, SpringerBriefs in Entrepreneurship and Innovation, https://doi.org/10.1007/978-3-030-53103-4

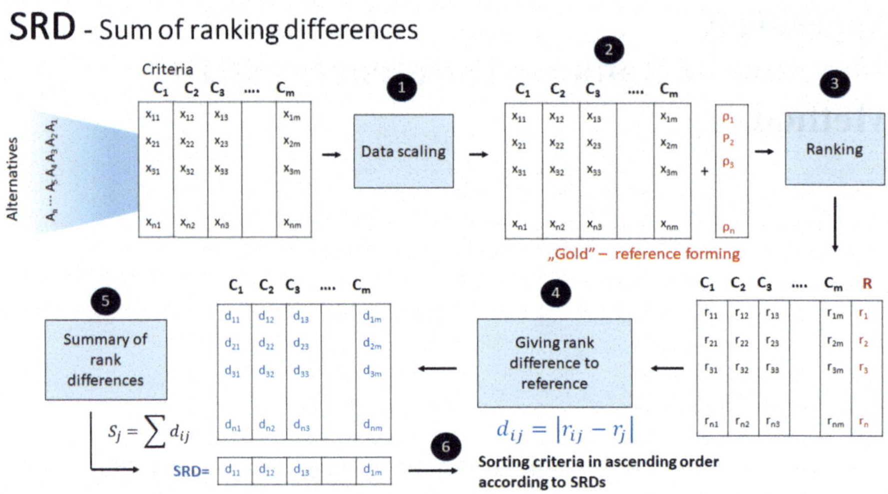

Fig. A.1 Methodological steps of SRD

Appendix B
The Promethee II Method

This chapter presents the methodology of Promethee II used for the integration of the individual I40+-specific measures.

Promethee II is a preference ranking organization method for enrichment evaluation, the steps of which are shown in Fig. B.1. Regarding the definition of Brans and Mareschal, Promethee is addressed to tackle multi criteria problems based on the following:

$$max\{g_1(a), g_2(a), \ldots, g_n(a)|a \in A\} \tag{B.1}$$

A donates the finite set of possible alternatives $\{a_1, a_2, \ldots, a_m\}$ and G represents a set of evaluation criteria (either maximized or minimized) $\{g_1(.), g_2(.), \ldots, g_n(.)\}$. Making an evaluation table is an essential step as shown in Table B.1:

The second row shows the weights of each criteria. The equation presents it clearly:

$$\sum_{j=1}^{n} \omega_j = 1, \quad j = 1, 2, \ldots, n \tag{B.2}$$

The preference degree in the case of Promethee refers to how an is preferred against another. So if the criterion is maximized, the preference number can be defined as:

$$P_j(a, b) = F_j[d_j(a, b)], \quad \forall a, b \in A \tag{B.3}$$

where $d_j(a, b)$ donates the difference in evaluation of the two actions (pairwise comparison)

$$d_j(a, b) = g_j(a) - g_j(b) \tag{B.4}$$

J. Abonyi et al., *Are Regions Prepared for Industry 4.0?*, SpringerBriefs in Entrepreneurship and Innovation, https://doi.org/10.1007/978-3-030-53103-4

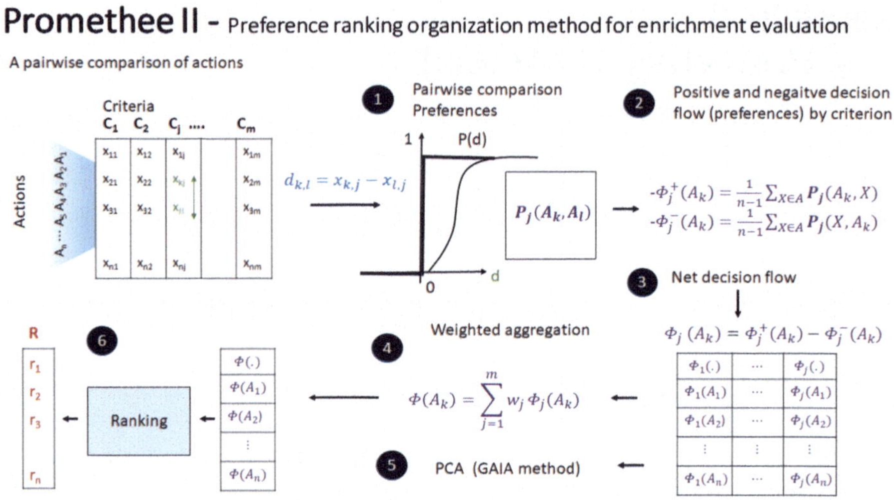

Fig. B.1 The methodological steps of Promethee II

Table B.1 Evaluation table

a	$g_1(.)$	$g_2(.)$	$\ldots$	$g_n(.)$
	w_1	w_2	$\ldots$	w_n
a_1	$g_1(a_1)$	$g_2(a_1)$	$\ldots$	$g_n(a_1)$
a_2	$g_1(a_2)$	$g_2(a_2)$	$\ldots$	$g_n(a_2)$
.	.	.	.	.
.	.	.	.	.
a_m	$g_1(a_m)$	$g_2(a_m)$	$\ldots$	$g_n(a_m)$

and the preference degree is a real number between 0 and 1:

$$0 \leq P_j(a, b) \leq 1 \tag{B.5}$$

If criterion g has to be minimized, then $-g$ has to be maximized. The aggregated preference indices are calculated as follows:

$$\begin{cases} \pi(a, b) = \sum_{j=1}^{n} P_j(a, b)\omega_j \\ \pi(b, a) = \sum_{j=1}^{n} P_j(a, b)\omega_j \end{cases} \tag{B.6}$$

$(a, b) \in A$, and $\pi(a, b)$ show how much action a is preferred to over b for the criteria, while $\pi(b, a)$ shows the opposite, i.e. how much action b is preferred to over a. The following properties are true for all values of $(a, b) \in A$:

$$\begin{cases} \pi(a,a) = 0 \\ 0 \leq \pi(a,b) \leq 1 \\ 0 \leq \pi(b,a) \leq 1 \\ 0 \leq \pi(a,b) + \pi(b,a) \leq 1 \end{cases} \tag{B.7}$$

Actions compete against (m−1) other actions in the set of A. The unicriterion positive flow in A of each action is a number between 0 and 1, which shows how much this action is preferred over all the others in A. Higher values refer to a more preferable action for the decision-maker. The positive outranking flow is defined as the following:

$$\phi^{+}(a) = \frac{1}{m-1} \sum_{x \in A} \pi(a,x) \tag{B.8}$$

In comparison, the negative outranking flow is an indicator which shows how all the other actions are preferred over one particular action and in accordance with the positive flow is defined as:

$$\phi^{-}(a) = \frac{1}{m-1} \sum_{x \in A} \pi(a,x) \tag{B.9}$$

The Gaia Method is a visual decision aid, which provides a representation of the ϕ matrix, where $i = 1, 2, \ldots, m$ and $j = 1, 2, \ldots, n$ in $\mathbb{R}^n$ based on the Principal Component Analysis technique (PCA). It aims to visualize the decision problems in two dimensions as shown in Fig. 4.5. To appropriately interpret the image, decision-makers should keep the following rules:

- The criteria are represented by axes.
- The length of each axes is remarkable (deviations from the evaluations of the actions in a defined criterion.) The larger the deviations of the net flow values, the longer the axis.
- The decision-maker has to consider the orientation of the criteria axis, as it refers to the "agreement" or "conflict" between the criteria. Criteria correlate if the angle between the axes is rather small, while if the angle is large, a conflict among the criteria exists which has to be taken into account.
- Actions are represented by dots and their profiles are implied by their relative positions. The indifference and preference thresholds are critical in defining the concept of similarity.

Appendix C
Description of Variables of the I4.0+ Indicator System

This chapter provides a summary of description of variables. Each variables measure at NUTS 2 spatial level. Tables C.1 and C.2 indicate the composition of indicators according to their field of measure.

J. Abonyi et al., *Are Regions Prepared for Industry 4.0?*, SpringerBriefs in Entrepreneurship and Innovation, https://doi.org/10.1007/978-3-030-53103-4

Table C.1 Description of variables I

Variables	
Population aged 25–64 by educational attainment level, sex and NUTS 2 regions (%) (edat_lfse_04)	
Age:	24–64
Educational attainment level:	ED0-2 Less than primary, primary and lower secondary education (levels 0–2)
	ED3-8 Upper secondary, post-secondary non-tertiary and tertiary education (levels 3–8)
	ED3_4 Upper secondary and post-secondary non-tertiary education (levels 3 and 4)
	ED5-8 Tertiary education (levels 5–8)
Sex:	T—Total
	M—Male
	F—Female
Unit:	PC—percentage
Population aged 30–34 by educational attainment level, sex and NUTS 2 regions (%) (edat_lfse_12)	
Age:	30–34
Educational attainment level:	ED0-2 Less than primary, primary and lower secondary education (levels 0–2)
	ED3-8 Upper secondary, post-secondary non-tertiary and tertiary education (levels 3–8)
	ED3_4 Upper secondary and post-secondary non-tertiary education (levels 3 and 4)
	ED3_4GEN Upper secondary and post-secondary non-tertiary education (levels 3 and 4)—general
	ED3_4VOC Upper secondary and post-secondary non-tertiary education (levels 3 and 4)—vocational
	ED5-8 Tertiary education (levels 5–8)
Sex:	T—Total
	M—Male
	F—Female
Unit:	PC—percentage

(continued)

Table C.1 (continued)

Variables	
Employment rates of young people not in education and training by sex, educational attainment level, years since completion of highest level of education and NUTS 2 regions (edat_lfse_33)	
Sex:	T—Total
	M—Male
	F—Female
Educational attainment level:	ED0-2 Less than primary, primary and lower secondary education (levels 0–2)
	ED3-8 Upper secondary, post-secondary non-tertiary and tertiary education (levels 3–8)
	ED3_4 Upper secondary and post-secondary non-tertiary education (levels 3 and 4)
	ED3_4GEN Upper secondary and post-secondary non-tertiary education (levels 3 and 4)—general
	ED3_4VOC Upper secondary and post-secondary non-tertiary education (levels 3 and 4)—vocational
	ED5-8 Tertiary education (levels 5-8)
	NRP No Response
Duration	Y1–3: from 1 to 3 years
	Y_LE3: 3 years or less
	Y_GT3: over 3 years
	Y_LE5: 5 years or less
	T_GT5: over 5 years
Age:	15–34
	18–34
	20–34
Unit:	PC—percentage
Number of students participating in mobility programmes	
ERASMUS_FROM_COUNT	Number of students going from a university with Erasmus+ mobility program
ERASMUS_TO_COUNT	Number of students going to a university with Erasmus+ mobility program
GRID (Global Research Identifier Database)	
GRID_count	Density of institutions
GDELT (Global Data on Events, Location and Tone)	
GDELT_count	Density of I4.0 related media appearings

Table C.2 Description of variables II

Variables	
Number of students graduate in I4.0 field of education	
Graduates_at_ISCED_6- Natural_sciences_mathematics_and_statistics	Number of graduates in Natural sciences, Mathematics and Statistics (BSc, MSc, PhD)
Graduates_at_ISCED_6- Information_and_Communication_Technologies	Number of graduates in Information and Communication Technologies (BSc, MSc, PhD)
Graduates_at_ISCED_6- Engineering_manufacturing_and_construction	Number of graduates in Engineering, Manufacturing and Construction (BSc, MSc, PhD)
Human Resources in Science and Technology by category and NUTS 2 regions (hrst_st_rcat)	
Category:	HRST—Persons with tertiary education (ISCED) and/or employed in science and technology
	HRSTE—Persons with tertiary education (ISCED)
	HRSTO—Persons employed in science and technology
	HRSTC—Persons with tertiary education (ISCED) and employed in science and technology
	SE—Scientists and engineers
Unit:	THS—Thousand
	PC_POP
	PC_ACT
Employment in technology and knowledge-intensive sectors by NUTS 2 regions and sex (from 2008 onwards, NACE Rev. 2) (htec_emp_reg2)	
NACE code:	HTC—High-technology sectors (high-technology manufacturing and knowledge-intensive high-technology services)
	C—Manufacturing
	C_HTC_MH—High and medium high-technology manufacturing
	C_HTC_M—Medium high-technology manufacturing
	C_HTC—High-technology manufacturing
	C_LTC-_LM Low and medium low-technology manufacturing
	C_LTC-_M Medium low-technology manufacturing
	C_LTC—Low-technology manufacturing
	KIS—Total knowledge-intensive services
	KIS_HTC—Knowledge-intensive high-technology services
	M—Professional, scientific and technical activities
	P—Education
Sex:	T—Total
Unit:	THS—Thousand
	PC_EMP—Percentage of total employment

(continued)

Table C.2 (continued)

Variables	
Publications by categories (I40Papers)	
Number of publications (at least two I4.0-related topic included)	Industrial engineering, Operations management, Process engineering, Transport engineering, Operations research, Simulation,Knowledge management, Control theory, Telecommunications,
	Mechanical engineering, Computer engineering, Software engineering, Manufacturing engineering,
	Machine learning, Data mining, Mathematical optimization, Control engineering, Regional science,
	Embedded system, Artificial intelligence, Process management, Reliability engineering, Systems engineering, Management science, Data science
Patents (I40_patent_count)	
Number of patent applications in the relevant field by regions	Additive manufacturing technology, Nanotechnology, Machines or engines in general; Engine plants in general; Steam engines, Controlling; Regulating, Computing; Calculating, Counting, Signaling, Information and communication technology (ICT) specially adapted for specific application fields
Intramural R&D expenditure (GERD) by sectors of performance and NUTS 2 regions (rd_e_gerdreg)	
Sector:	BES—Business enterprise sector
	GOV—Government sector
	HES—Higher education sector
	PNP—Private non-profit sector
Unit:	PC_GDP—Percentage of gross domestic product (GDP)
Total R&D personnel and researchers by sectors of performance, sex and NUTS 2 regions (rd_p_persreg)	
Sex:	T—Total
Professional position:	T—Total
	RSE—Researchers
Sector:	BES—Business enterprise sector
	GOV—Government sector
	HES—Higher education sector
	PNP—Private non-profit sector
Unit:	HC—Head Count
	PC_EMP_FTE—Percentage of total employment—numerator in full-time equivalent (FTE)

Index

J. Abonyi et al., *Are Regions Prepared for Industry 4.0?*, SpringerBriefs in Entrepreneurship and Innovation, https://doi.org/10.1007/978-3-030-53103-4

The manufacturer's authorised representative in the EU is Springer Nature Customer Service Centre GmbH, Europaplatz 3, 69115 Heidelberg, Germany. If you have any concerns regarding our products, please contact ProductSafety@springernature.com

Printed and bound by CPI Group (UK) Ltd, Croydon, CR0 4YY
22/09/2026
02221059-0015